TWO THOUSAND YEARS OF
CHRISTIANITY AND IRELAND

Edited by John R. Bartlett and Stuart D. Kinsella

Two Thousand Years of Christianity and Ireland

LECTURES DELIVERED IN CHRIST CHURCH CATHEDRAL, DUBLIN, 2001-2002

the columba press

First published in 2006 by
the columba press
55A Spruce Avenue, Stillorgan Industrial Park,
Blackrock, Co Dublin

Cover by Bill Bolger
Origination by The Columba Press
Printed in Ireland by ColourBooks Ltd, Dublin

ISBN 1 85607 526 5

Table of Contents

Introduction

The origins of this book lie in a series of lunchtime lectures given at Christ Church Cathedral in Dublin. They form part of a continual fostering of public curiosity in the history, traditions and future direction of both the Cathedral and the surrounding city. The concept of '2000 years of Christianity in Ireland' first arose in September 2000 as a millennial project. The original proposal was for a course of twenty lectures, but wise counsel from the cathedral's Archives, Information Technology and Education Committee suggested the more modest pattern of integrating them into the 'Christ Church Lecture Series', lunchtime lectures which have run since 1997. Not until May 2001 did plans solidify, but, once arranged, the lectures ran successfully in October 2001, February 2002 and May 2002, as the 11th, 12th, and 13th sets of the series, and were rewardingly attended. If the emphasis of the papers occasionally drifts towards the cathedral and local Dublin examples, this was largely for the benefit of a lunchtime audience listening attentively in the atmospheric setting of a darkened cathedral crypt.

For the smooth running of the lectures and for the hospitable atmosphere created afterwards, special thanks are due to the cathedral staff including former cathedral manager, Mark Bowyer, former press officer, Sheila Kulkarni and the head verger, Kieran O'Reilly. The assistance of the members of the Archives (now Culture) committee, was also invaluable, particularly that of Dr Kenneth Milne, chairman, and Dr Raymond Refaussé, librarian and archivist of the Representative Church Body Library. Of particular added benefit was the symbiotic relationship nourished between Dublin City Council and the cathedral by city archivist, Mary Clark, which facilitated the joint advertising of a number of city centre lectures in both Christ Church and the City Hall.

Inevitably the book differs slightly from its original conception. It was unfortunately not possible to include the lectures given by Dr Ailbhe MacShamhráin ('The monastic organisation of the Irish church with reference to Glendalough') and Dr James Murray ('The dawn of the Reformation in Ireland'), and we are grateful to Professor Colm Lennon for filling one particular lacuna. We are also grateful to the current editor of *Search*, the Revd Canon Dr K.V. Kennerley, for permission to reproduce the article by Andrew Pierce here. While this volume is by no means alone in attempting the impossible task of summarising 2000 years of Christianity in a single volume, we trust that there is merit in shedding new light on the subject from an Irish perspective. Indeed Seán O Boyle and The Columba Press, to whom we are most grateful for taking on this publication, have already blazed the trail in publishing the proceedings of a similarly themed conference in Italy in 1999: Brendan Bradshaw and Dáire Keogh (eds.), *Christianity in Ireland: revisiting the story* (2002). We are grateful to Richard Griffiths for help with the Index.

In a world ever more polarised by religious conflict, one modest hope of this book is that, in the following pages, the inquisitive non-specialist might be urged to delve into the myriad complexities of over two millennia of religious history and culture, and explore the fascinating and often surprising origins from which today's society has emerged.

The Editors
St Patrick's Day, March 2006

The Birth of Christianity and the Christianisation of the Empire

Seán Freyne

'In the fifteenth year of the Emperor Tiberius, when Pontius Pilate was governor of Judea and Herod (Antipas) was tetrarch of Galilee and his brother Philip was tetrarch of the region of Iturea and Trachonitis, and Lysanias ruler of Abilene, during the high-priesthood of Annas and Caiaphas, the word of God came to John, the son of Zechariah in the wilderness' (Lk 3:1-2).

The Evangelist Luke introduces the public ministry of John the Baptist with this sweeping chronological summary that includes within its purview both Roman imperial and provincial rulers as well as occupants of the Jewish high-priestly office. Luke clearly wanted to stress both the worldwide and local implications of the ministry of Jesus which he is about to narrate. It is fair to say that not even Luke, despite his confident account of the rise and spread of early Christianity, could have anticipated just how successful that movement was going to be as he traced its inexorable progress from Galilee, via Jerusalem to Rome in his two-volume work, comprising the gospel and Acts of the Apostles. While Luke, along with other early Christian writers, presented Jesus' coming as 'good news' for the world, the fact is that from the very beginning this new movement provided a serious challenge to both Roman imperial values and Jewish religious institutions, drawing its inspiration from Jewish messianic hopes, as these were seen to apply to Jesus' career. Within the space of less than three hundred years, and in spite of repeated persecution, the Christian religion had spread throughout the empire, east and west, and had penetrated every level of society. Such was the extent of its progress that Constantine, in search of a unifying force for the divided empire after his victory over his imperial rival in 312 CE, decided for Christianity as the most viable option.

The Beginnings of Christianity

It is customary to describe Jesus as the founder of Christianity, but such a designation is in danger of distorting the reality. The Jesus-as-founder idea suggests that he intended to establish a new religion independently of his own Jewish heritage. However, the fact is that Jesus lived and died as a Jewish prophet from Galilee who regarded his own public ministry of word and work as the inauguration of God's kingly rule in the world, as this had been envisaged in the Jewish scriptures. For three centuries prior to Jesus the Jews of Palestine had experienced domination by various world empires – Persia, Greece, Rome – thus heightening the hopes that their God's universal rule would soon be established. This expectation set in train various scenarios of restoration and redemption among different strands of the Jewish people. Jesus too shared such hopes, but unlike some of his contemporaries, who believed that God's kingdom would be established through violent revolution, he saw its advent differently. God's kingly rule would be God's doing. Humans were called on to recognise and acknowledge its presence in Jesus' inclusive ministry of healing and caring for the outcasts among his contemporaries, a far cry from the apocalyptic upheavals that many expected.

It is difficult to be more specific as to the origins of Jesus' distinctive view of God's kingdom and his own role in regard to its advent, given the nature of our sources and the absence of any information in regard to the 'hidden years'. When he does emerge from the obscurity of a village craftsman it is as a disciple of John the Baptist that he enters the stage of history. John also was expecting the imminent arrival of God's kingdom with his preaching about judgement on the wicked and the need for repentance: 'Now the axe is laid to the root of the tree,' he insisted, highlighting the urgency of the present moment. Jesus on the other hand had come to see the present as a time of God's gracious, but hidden presence in the world and his ministry consisted in giving expression to that graciousness in terms of healing the broken and freeing those who were captive, in accordance with the great Jubilee hopes of Israel (Isa 61:1-2; Mt 11:2-5; Lk 4:18-19).

The contrast between Jesus' active ministry in the Galilean villages and John's stark message of judgement is striking, given their close association earlier. In Galilee Jesus encountered imperial rule at first hand. As a young adult he would have seen Sepphoris, just 4 kms from his native Nazareth, being rebuilt and renamed in order to honour the Roman emperor as sole ruler, by the Herod Antipas. Less than 30 kms away on the lakefront, a new city, Tiberias, was also founded for the same purpose in 19 CE. Antipas' father, Herod the Great, had begun the policy of honouring his Roman patrons but most of his monumental buildings were in the south. Now, however, Antipas, who aspired to succeed his father as king, was anxious to win favour by following the same policy in his building projects in Galilee, albeit on a more modest scale.

It would appear that the immediate catalyst for Jesus' ministry, with its different emphasis from that of John, was the rapidly changing social and economic situation that was occurring in Galilee when he returned there after John's arrest and subsequent murder. This does not of course exclude other, more long-term factors such as domination by external powers and the deleterious effects that such circumstances had had on Jewish religious life and practice for centuries. Nevertheless, the establishment of a city in the immediate neighbourhood of his own village must have involved a serious disruption to all aspects of life in the region as a whole. A new and often alien element was introduced into the population of the region, involving confiscation of the land of the native population. The new arrivals would normally be representatives of the retainer classes – scribes, tax-collectors, military personnel, including army veterans – all supporting the regime in return for the various favours they would have received. Their main function was to ensure that sufficient revenue was extracted annually from the peasants to ensure the opulent lifestyle of the elites, local, provincial and imperial, that constituted the pyramid of power in Roman Galilee, as elsewhere in the Near East, was maintained.

It is surely significant that Jesus is never said to have visited

Sepphoris or Tiberias within Galilee. Nor did he visit any of the major cities in the surrounding regions, but only 'the borders of Tyre', 'the villages of Caesarea Philippi' and 'the territory of the Dekapolis'. This strategy cannot be explained by a policy of cautious evasion or undercover activity away from the eyes of the ruling elite, given Jesus public stance otherwise. 'Render to Caesar what is Caesar's and to God what is God's' (Mk 12:7), must be understood as a defiant, not a compliant statement. His ministry can be seen as a throwing down of the gauntlet to the value-systems of both the Roman ruling elite and the Jewish priestly classes. Nowhere is his attitude more clearly expressed than in the encomium for his mentor, John. 'What did you go out to the desert to see? A reed shaken by the wind?' Some scholars think that this rhetorical question is a veiled reference to Antipas, whose coins bore the emblem of a palm tree. Whatever about this suggestion, the subsequent reference to 'royal palaces' and 'fine garments' can only have been directed at the elite residents of the Herodian cities as far as Jesus and his audiences were concerned (Mt 11:7-10). Jesus, like John, had nothing to do with such ostentatious opulence that was so far-removed from the Galilean peasants with whose lifestyle and daily struggle he was so familiar. The many 'real life' images and situations that are represented in his parables show just how close he is to the ordinary lives of people. These images, culled from the everyday lives of his Galilean peasant neigh-bours and from the Galilean landscape, spoke to him more im-mediately and directly about God than did those taken from the splendour of Near Eastern royalty, which, even within his own Jewish tradition, were most frequently employed to speak of God's universal rule.

We can catch a glimpse of Jesus' alternative vision that was as shocking to many of his own co-religionists as it was to Roman elites, by reading it in the context both of Rome's own ideology of universal rule as expressed, e.g. in Virgil's Fourth Eclogue, and the hopes which Jewish poets and prophets had expressed for the coming messianic age (Isa 9:1-6; 11:1-11).

These hopes were, like Rome's, based on the idea of universal rule where peace and harmony would prevail between all humans and with the natural world as well. The 'new creation' was to be a restoration of the world to God's original plan, where human domination, greed, and exploitation would be eliminated and the good things of the earth would be shared as gifts for all, and were not deemed to be the prerogative of the few. In this process of restoration Israel was called on to play a special role – 'the light of the nations' – by witnessing to the possibilities that such a life offered to all, rather than seeking to dominate others.

There were many variants to this picture among Jesus' contemporaries, and different groups such as the Zealots and Essenes had different strategies for the implementation of their particular vision. Such reformist groups shared with Jesus a critical stance with regard to the Jewish religious establishment, which had increasingly opted to collaborate with the imperial powers, and in so doing to imitate their values. While sharing the dissatisfaction of other dissident groups with regard to the central institutions of their religion, the Jesus-movement developed its own strategy, namely, the adoption of a lifestyle and values-system that were the direct antithesis of those of the Roman aristocratic and Jewish priestly classes. This alternative was not merely envisaged but lived out in the context of Jesus' and his permanent followers' activity in Galilee. The radical rejection of family, possessions and reputation, which is the hallmark of the Jesus-movement, is a striking statement in action of what Jesus' understanding of God's rule was and the kind of demands that it made. 'Blessed are the poor' is not just a pious sentiment of resignation to the realities of 'meritocracies' but a defiant protest that those who judge blessings by power and possessions are deluded. Unlike others of their contemporaries his teaching was expressed through deeds more than through words. His lifestyle was intended as a statement of his own worldview. The kingdom of God was for Jesus a vocation, not an idea.

Unlike his mentor, John the Baptist, Jesus did not fall foul of

Antipas in Galilee. Indeed Antipas is singularly absent from the story of the Galilean ministry of Jesus, other than the mention in Luke that Jesus was warned by some Pharisees of Herod's (Antipas) desire to kill him (Lk 13:31). Jesus' defiant reply does not suggest any strategy of avoidance on his part, but rather a reaffirmation of his own sense of vocation to continue the prophetic ministry that would eventually take him to Jerusalem, the centre of his own religious tradition. However, according to the prophetic voices of Ezekiel, Jeremiah, but especially Isaiah, that centre was to be the focal point of restoration, not just for Israel, but for the nations also. There can be little doubt that this overall picture corresponds to the reality of Jesus' actual ministry, something that was important to Luke, as he stresses in the prologue to his gospel (Lk 1:1-4). Certainly, Luke is the most explicit in describing Jesus' activity in political terms: he was arrested and tried as a disturber of the peace, 'beginning from Galilee to this place' (Lk 23:2.5). Thus, while the language and colouring may be Luke's, the independent attestation from the Jewish historian Josephus (*Antiquities*, 18. 63), corroborating that of all the evangelists, that Jesus was crucified by Pilate, is a clear indication that he was viewed as a political threat both by the Roman authorities and the Jewish ruling elite. It should be remembered that crucifixion was reserved by the Romans for those who were deemed to be not merely criminal, but a danger to the well-being of Rome itself.

From Jesus to Constantine
Many scholars have attempted to explain the rapid spread of the early Christian movement within the Greco-Roman world by comparing it to other religious movements of the time. In particular the mystery religions were seen as providing the best comparison, since various aspects of the new movement as it appears in the letters of Paul, for example, would seem to have a close resemblance to the cults of Isis, Dionysus and Mithras, among others. These similarities range from initiation rites to sacred meals and mythological accounts of the ways in which

the respective heroes achieved divine status. In this view, it was Paul, not Jesus who should be seen as the real founder of Christianity. However, this version of events has come in for serious criticism as scholars have begun to rediscover the importance of the memory of the historical Jesus for the first Christians, after a period of deep scepticism about the possibility of retrieving that elusive figure. Paul, far from seeing himself as the founder of a new movement, declared that anyone who proclaimed a gospel other than the one that he proclaimed, should be deemed accursed (Gal 1:9). He shared with Jesus the hopes of Jewish restoration, which included not just the renewal of Israel but also the ingathering of the nations into the one human family.

Not that we should consider the Christian movement as being a seamless robe from the outset. Luke's account in *Acts of the Apostles* suggests an idyllic period of unity that gradually became disrupted through an apparently trivial dispute between the Hebrews and the Hellenists. These groups are seen as representing two culturally diverse tendencies within the primitive Christian community in Jerusalem, and the expulsion of the former, following the martyrdom of Stephen leads to the beginnings of the mission to the gentiles (Acts 6-8; 11). Because of Luke's particular interest in describing the contribution of Paul, who himself was also a Hellenist, to the development of the early Christian mission, students of early Christianity have tended to ignore the role of the Hebrews, who are often portrayed as conservative and xenophobic. However, this is to misunderstand the significance of their role in establishing a permanent community in Jerusalem. The leader of that group was James the brother of the Lord, whose pivotal role is merely hinted at within the New Testament, primarily in terms of providing a compromise between the law-free mission of Paul and judaising Christians who were insisting on the necessity of circumcision for Paul's gentile converts (Acts 15:13-21; Gal 1:19; 2:9f)

More important than this mediating role is the fact that both Hebrews and Hellenists alike share a sense of the universal mission of the new movement, based on the memory and practice of

Jesus, a universalism that was already part of the prophetic tradition of Israel, as previously noted. Thus, while Jerusalem was to
remain central to the hopes of all those – Hebrews and
Hellenists within the first generation after Jesus – who followed
the Isaian declaration that Wisdom would go forth from Zion,
gradually the centre of gravity of the movement was to shift.
The destruction of the Jerusalem temple by the Romans in 70 CE
was a shock to the religious sensibilities of messianic Jews
(Christians/Nazarenes), as well as non-messianic Jews alike. A
token group from the Jesus-movement may have returned to
Jerusalem in the early second century, as later church historians
seem to imply. Yet, in an increasingly hostile environment
among the various strands of post-70 Judaism, the destruction of
the city and the temple came to be interpreted as God's punish-
ment on the temple and its personnel, and Christian writers
began to speak of the new and heavenly Jerusalem rather than
the earthly one (*Epistle to the Hebrews* and the *Revelation of John*).
Antioch, Alexandria and Rome, the great cultural and political
centres of the Mediterranean world, were to become the new
centres, instead.

Unfortunately, we cannot trace in any detail the progress of
the Jerusalem-based Christianity of the earlier period, even
though various groups such as the Nazarenes, and the Ebionites
have been located in the Transjordan region according to later
writers. It may be that it was from such groups as these that
Syriac Christianity, with its distinctive literary and liturgical
traditions, emanated. Indeed it has been speculated that the very
positive treatment of both Jesus and Mary in the Qur'an is due to
the fact that several early Christian communities in that region
joined the new religion as Islam expanded north and east in the
seventh century CE.

Many different explanations have been given for the success
of the Christian mission within the Roman Empire, a success
that was by no means obvious even as late as the end of the second century. Indeed it is possible to trace a line of thinking within early Christian writing that sees the Roman Empire as evil

and seeks to reject it and all that it stands for. This is most famously expressed in the *Revelation of John*, where the author engages in a mock lament for the fall of Rome that he predicts as imminent (Rev 18). Almost a century later, Tertullian, himself a convert to Christianity in adult life having been trained as a lawyer, wrote defensively but self-confidently about Christian attitudes to Rome:

> What indeed has Athens to do with Jerusalem? What has the Academy to do with the Church? What have heretics to do with Christians? Our instruction comes from the porch of Solomon, who had himself taught that the Lord should be sought in simplicity of heart. Away with all attempts to produce a Stoic, a Platonic or a dialectic Christianity. We want no curious disputation after receiving the gospel.
> (*De Praescriptione Haereticorum* 7.9).

Despite these expressions of hostility, there are clear indications that other attitudes could be and were expressed that gradually changed the character of the early Christian worldview from an apocalyptically inspired rejection of the world to one that sought to transform the present world, while also affirming the goodness of the created order. Such a shift is not as dramatic as might appear, given the fact that in the Jewish heritage itself, both wisdom and apocalyptic are often combined, expressing on the one hand the goodness of God's creation, while concurrently longing for a new age when evil in all its manifestations would be destroyed. Expressions of rejection of the world, such as those mentioned above, are usually made in contexts of open hostility when the new movement was being persecuted and martyrdom was seen as a glorious crown in imitation of the founder Jesus, who was put to death unjustly by Roman power, but who subsequently was vindicated by God. As early as Paul, one finds this ambivalence being expressed. On the one hand he warns his Christian readers that they cannot drink of the cup of the Lord and the cup of demons (1 Cor 10:21), and in the same letter he can claim that his own strategy meant being Jew to the Jews and Greek to the Greeks (1 Cor 9:19-23).

His readers are exhorted not to abandon this world, even if it
meant having to deal with immoral people (1 Cor 5:11). Even
Tertullian, whose forthright views have just been cited, can
speak of the Roman philosopher Seneca as *'saepe noster'*, that is,
'often one of our own' since he agreed with his Stoic philosophi-
cal ideas (*De Anima* 10).

It is against this background that one has to evaluate the success of the early Christian missionary experience within the
Greco-Roman world. The capacity to be inculturated into that
society would appear to have been of paramount importance,
while at the same time refusing to bow to imperial and social
pressures when challenged during the various persecutions of
the second and third centuries CE. Undoubtedly, the Christian
movement raised Roman patrician suspicion of all eastern cults
that found their way to the city, but it soon became apparent that
this new cult was somehow different, and ultimately the threat
that it posed to Roman values came to be recognised. It was a
pernicious *superstitio* that allegedly engaged in all kinds of illicit
practices, even cannibalism, according to the imperial rhetoric of
vilification (Pliny's *Letter to Trajan*, X. 96). The Christian response in the early apologists, such as Quadratus, Aristeides,
Justin Martyr and Irenaeus, was to claim that Christianity was a
vera philosophia, often backing up the assertion with an eclectic
approach to the various popular philosophies of the day
(Stoicism and Cynicism in particular), especially when it was
convenient to draw on the writings of these schools to elucidate
the Christian way of life. This meant that the appeal of Christianity
was not just among the underprivileged masses of the empire. It
began to address the educated elites also, thereby striking a
blow at the very heart of the imperial ideology.

Another factor of importance to the success of the Christians
was the historical figure of Jesus. Unlike Heracles, Dionysus,
Asklepius or Isis, who were venerated in the various mystery religions that flourished in the early centuries, Jesus was a person
of flesh and blood. The gospels, for all their later theological reflection and differing perspectives, were anchored in the real

world of time and space, an aspect that Luke in particular seeks to underline in his narrative account. Nothing illustrates better the significance of this dimension of the early Christian success than the fact that a counter-propaganda was initiated not just by Jews but by pagans also to discredit Jesus. The attack was not aimed at his alleged mythological status but rather at his human characteristics, thus adopting the strategy of political vilification which highlighted such aspects of an opponent as ignoble birth, lowly status and dubious conduct.

The Christian theologian, Origen of Alexandria, wrote a defence of Christianity in the early third century CE. His work, *Contra Celsum*, is a detailed refutation of such claims made by a pagan writer, Celsus, some fifty years earlier, who introduced a fictitious Jewish figure to challenge the veracity of the gospels' accounts about Jesus. Origen uses his superior knowledge of Judaism to refute the claims of Celsus' Jew, showing him to be ignorant of his own tradition and pointing to the moral character of Jesus' teaching to reject the claim that he was a deceiver and a fraud. Even among Christians there were in circulation views about Jesus, other than those represented in the canonical or official versions of his life (those of Matthew, Mark, Luke and John). Since the discovery in 1947 at Nag Hammadi in Egypt of some of the writings belonging to those whom the Christian apologists, such as Irenaeus, had described as heretical, we are in a better position to understand the worldview of those generally labelled Gnostics. Their spirituality was based on a combination of Platonic views of knowledge as illumination and accounts of Jesus which stress his post-Resurrection status as Revealer of the truth. This emphasis was at the expense of the narrative accounts of his solidarity with the poor and the marginalised of this world. Aspects of the Gnostics' philosophy were indeed highly attractive in élite circles within the Empire, as we can now discern from the Gospel of Thomas and the Gospel of Truth. However, in the end it was the more established versions of the four-fold canonical accounts that won the day, and the Gnostic point of view receded from view as Catholic Christianity became the official religion of the Empire.

Another feature of the new movement that aided its expansion and growth is the sense of community that it engendered. Within its original Jewish matrix the Jesus movement was essentially communal in character, growing out of Jewish messianic hopes and aspirations. The emergence of the household as the key social setting where the new movement took root in an urban environment helped to reinforce the sense of its togetherness. What have been described as fictive kinship groups were formed in which close ties of brotherhood and sisterhood were established, based on the shared belief in Jesus' divine status and a common value system modelled on his lifestyle, as this was known through the gospel narratives. Unlike other such free associations in the Greco-Roman cities, such groups were part of a developing network that involved communication between the various groups across the Mediterranean region. Hospitality was an important dimension of the movement's ethos and a common style of worship in which the story of Jesus' life was remembered and celebrated, tended to sanction these ties and furnish them with greater legitimacy. Though informal at first, the development of structures of authority and leadership that were regional, and eventually universal, ensured a permanency that would not have been maintained otherwise.

On the larger front of the city as a Greco-Roman political institution of all the citizens, the choice of the term *ekklesia* as the favoured self-identifier of the group had a resonance also. This was the technical term for the general assembly of all free-born citizens within the *polis*, or city institution, and the Christian assembly was seen to be laying claims to a similar sense of solidarity and shared purpose. Indeed it was this image that was most frequently noted with suspicion by pagan detractors who saw the new movement as subversive and threatening to the well-being of Roman society. The refusal to offer sacrifice to the emperor only added to these suspicions, leading often to bitter persecution. Far from dissuading Christian converts from professing their new religion, however, these persecutions created a greater sense of purpose and fostered the desire for martyrdom, which was to become the ideal and crown of the Christian life. Martyrdom was not a desire to flee the world, but rather to emulate the witness of Jesus who dared to challenge the might of Rome and was vindicated by God for doing so.

This dimension of the Christian movement is closely related to another important element in its success within the larger Greco-Roman world, namely its attitude to death. The second century CE has been described as 'an age of anxiety', meaning that at all levels of society there was a growing unease about the purpose and destiny of human life. This would explain the marked increase in the appeal of the various mystery religions already alluded to, each of them offering a more personal contact with the divine world than that of the official state religion of Emperor worship. As early as the apostle Paul, this aspect of Christian belief was deemed to be highly important. Writing to the Thessalonians he reminds them that they are not like their pagan neighbours 'who have no hope' in the face of the death of loved ones (1 Thess 4:13). Paul and his Christian converts can challenge death: 'Death where is your victory? Death where is your sting?' he proclaims, almost tauntingly, as he contemplates the consequences for believers of Christ's victory in the resurrection (1 Cor 15:54f). One has only to consider the early Christian art as this appears in the catacombs to catch a glimpse of this confident hope of Christian believers. Stories such as Jonah in the whale's belly, the sacrifice of Isaac and Daniel in the lion's den provide the inspiration for this art, all of them pointing to God's care in rescuing his own from life-threatening dangers. In a world where burial guilds, which guaranteed remembrance of a kind for their members after death, were such a frequent feature of Roman urban life, the Christian claims were both attractive and consoling.

The Emergence of a Christian Empire

The precarious situation of the Christian church throughout the second and third centuries was to change dramatically in the early fourth century. Constantine's victory over his rivals for the

sole rule of the empire, east and west, at the battle of the Milvian
Bridge, close to Rome, in 312 CE was indeed a watershed for
both the empire and the church. Much has been written about
his alleged vision of the cross on the eve of the battle with the as-
surance that 'in this sign you will conquer'. Did Constantine
have a Pauline conversion experience, or was his decision to opt
for the Christian religion as the one most likely to bring peace
and unity of a kind to the empire, merely strategic? The evidence would seem to point in the latter direction. Not merely did
his coins continue to have representations of Apollo, the Sun
God, after the victory, but even the famous Edict of Milan issued
in 314 CE, did not immediately make Christianity the official
state religion, merely promising toleration to all, including
Christians to worship their God freely and publicly.

While Constantine's own piety might be called into question,
at least in the early stages of his reign, he certainly saw to it that
the Christian church would play its part in his plans for the empire. As is well known, the Emperor involved himself personally
in the conduct of affairs at the Council of Nicea in 324 CE, thereby
insuring that Trinitarian theological disputes about the relation
between the Father and the Son would not spill over into political divisions within the new religion. By the sheer dint of numbers Christians had attained such a level of social and political
importance that their internal disputes could be disruptive of
the whole social and political fabric of the empire. Slowly but
surely, the privileged position of the Christian religion as the
state religion began to manifest itself in various legal enactments, often directed at restricting the ancient rights and privileges under Roman law of the Jews. The writings of the
Christian theologian and historiographer, Eusebius, bishop of
Caesarea in Palestine, are particularly informative in terms of
changed Christian attitudes towards the emperor. From being
the terrifying Beast of the Apocalypse at the end of the first century, he had become God's agent to save the new religion, virtually a new embodiment of the eternal *Logos*. There was a deep
irony about this change of fortune for Jews and Christians. For a

religious movement that had begun as a Jewish protest movement against Roman values, and which had suffered greatly at
the hands of various emperors, Christianity had suddenly become the favoured child. This change of status meant that the
mother religion, Judaism, was about to undergo increasing
marginalisation in terms of its legal protection and its freedom
of expression within an increasingly Christian empire.

Nowhere was this change more apparent than in the changing landscape of Palestine itself. Whereas previously Christian
eyes had been directed to the new and heavenly Jerusalem, they
now turned their attention to the actual Jerusalem, or *Aelia
Capitolina*, as pagan Jerusalem had been called since the time of
Hadrian (135 CE). Helena, the emperor's mother had visited the
Holy Land in 329 CE, shortly before her death, out of a genuine
desire to visit the place where the Saviour had lived and died.
Constantine thereafter decided to honour those places also.
Previous emperors had built temples to honour the pagan gods
in various cities, but now the Christian emperor set about honouring the God under whose sign he had conquered by the erection of churches and other monuments. Rome, his new capital,
Constantinople, and then Jerusalem were the beneficiaries of his
benevolence. According to Eusebius, he was determined to
adorn Jerusalem as a 'memorial' and 'sign' of Christ's death and
its efficacy. 'Contrary to every expectation' the cave of Jesus'
burial was discovered directly beneath a pagan temple, and it
was on this site that the church of the *Anastasis* or Resurrection
was built to a manner that 'would surpass the most beautiful
buildings in every city'. Soon other churches adorned various
sites associated with Jesus' life – the Mount of Olives, Bethlehem
and Nazareth, and this tradition was continued by succeeding
emperors, culminating in the great Nea church built by the emperor Justinian in 543 CE. Pilgrims flocked to the holy land and
Christian monks from the west built their monasteries in the
Judean desert close to the holy city. These buildings represented
the triumph of Christianity and their architecture was intended
to make a statement to that effect, a statement that was all the

more poignant because of the fact that the Temple Mount lay desolate, awaiting the arrival of the third Abrahamic faith, Islam, before it would again regain its former glory as a place of worship.

The age of Constantine was indeed a golden age – of a kind – for the Christian church. The prophecy of Isaiah that the lamb and the wolf would lie down together seemed to have been realised, and no doubt many fourth century Christians who had bitter memories of the imperial persecutions believed that to be the case. Whether or not the reconciliation was in the longer term interest of the Christian religion and its capacity to articulate the prophetic vision of Jesus, is indeed a moot point. Henceforth, the interest of empire and church were supposedly identical. Christian military crusades were undertaken against the new infidel without any thought as to whether these were genuine expressions of the spirit of him who said 'love your enemy'. The new millennium is surely a suitable moment to reflect on the need to de-imperialise the Christian church in the west as a way of recapturing something of the original prophetic voice of the Galilean.

Suggestions for further reading:
Chadwick, Henry, *The Early Church*, Harmondsworth: Penguin Books, 1967
-- *Early Christian Thought and the Classical Tradition*, Oxford: Clarendon Press, 1984
Freyne, Sean, *Texts, Contexts and Cultures*, Dublin: Veritas, 2002
-- *Jesus, a Jewish Galilean. A New Reading of the Jesus Story*, London and New York, Continuum, 2004.
MacMullen, Ramsay, *Christianizing the Roman Empire, A.D. 100-40*, London and New Haven, Yale University Press, 1984
Stephenson, J. ed., *A New Eusebius. Documents illustrative of the Church to A.D. 337*, London, S.P.C.K., 1974
Wilken, Robert, *The Christians as the Romans saw Them*, London and New Haven, Yale University Press, 1984
-- *The Land called Holy. Palestine in Christian History and Thought*, London and New Haven, Yale University Press, 1992

This lecture was originally delivered in a shorter form on 9 October 2001.

Patrick's conversion of Ireland to Christianity and the establishment of Armagh

Catherine Swift

My remit is to cover the thorny issues involved in the arrival of Christianity within Ireland and the establishment of the church settlement at Armagh. By way of introduction I should say that the following paper represents my personal assessment of the subject; there are a myriad of other possible views and the questions raised are still hotly debated. I use the word hotly advisedly; it was a long-suffering wife who once remarked in the early 70s that Patrician studies were a field in which no stone was left unthrown and many Patrician scholars today reiterate that comment with pride.

Arguments about Patrick's career and the scope of his mission have rumbled around the corridors of Irish academia since the days of Archbishop James Ussher in the seventeenth century. Much of this discourse is now limited to scholarly tomes but the one element which seems to have survived as part of popular folklore is the idea of the two Patricks, put forward by Professor T. F. O'Rahilly in 1954. This argument and indeed, the arguments about Patrick in general revolve, for the most part, around the problem of sources; apart from Patrick's own writings, the *Confessio* and the *Letter to Coroticus*, we have few sources which we can say are definitely fifth century in date. We have relatively plentiful sources, on the other hand, of later or indeed much later date, which purport to deal with fifth-century issues. Many scholars have tried to pick out the 'real' fifth-century facts from this later material while at the same time acknowledging that the bits which aren't real are propaganda for various church establishments.

One of the arguments behind the Two Patricks model, for example, is a reference in the *Annals of Ulster* to the elder Patrick who is said to have died in 457. If you have an elder, you must have a younger, and hey presto, you have two Patricks. The trouble with all these arguments is that it has involved a lot of cherry-picking – what one scholar sees as real, another sees as propaganda. It seems to me that dispassionate people, looking at the list of entries in the *Annals of Ulster* (including the four different dates for the saint's death), would have very little difficulty in acknowledging that Irish annalists were very interested in Patrick but they don't appear to have known much about him. And unfortunately, what is true for the annals is also true for the lives of St Patrick, which are seventh century or later in date.

Equally, there is little which seems inherently trustworthy about the claims of saints Ailbe of Emly, Déclán of Ardmore, Ibar of Beggary Island and Ciarán of Seirkieran to be missionaries in Ireland before St Patrick. These claims come, almost entirely, from a thirteenth-century collection of saints' lives which appear to have been put together by a Leinsterman. The saints in question were patrons of important southern churches for the most part and churches that disputed the claims of Armagh to primacy during much of the period before the Normans arrived. In other words, as historians we can see good reasons for identifying these claims as propaganda while the arguments for seeing them as 'fifth-century facts' boil down in the end to a matter of faith.

Some may be surprised that I have not included St Brigid in this list of pre-Patrician saints. Our medieval sources are unanimous in stating that Brigid, as the daughter of a druid, was a contemporary of Patrick who lived and worked in an Irish world where Christianity was well-known. She herself is not said to be a missionary although she did bring many to a Christian way of life by her example and through her miracles. The belief that she represents a pre-Christian goddess transformed into an Irish saint is very much the creation of modern scholarship and is heavily dependent on the fact that the element *brí* in her name is found fairly frequently in Roman sources, both in Britain and on the Continent.

While our Irish lives of the saints are largely concerned with figures who were patrons of powerful churches in the pre-Norman period, another characteristic feature is their lack of interest in the conversion process. Saints are described as meeting pagans, performing miracles and as a consequence, their over-awed audiences acknowledge the superiority of Christianity. It is only on very rare occasions that conversion is dealt with in a less stereotyped way. One such is the story about Patrick's arrival at Rathcroghan in Connacht, where two of the king of Tara's daughters were being fostered by druids. The two girls met Patrick and his retinue at the well, not knowing, so our author tells us, what people they belonged to, nor what region, nor whether they were men of the *síd* or other-world. They proceeded to ask them who they are and Patrick replied, that they should rather ask about God than about his race. In reply, the older girl made a speech:

> Who is God and where is God and whose God is he and where is his dwelling place? Has your God sons and daughters, gold and silver? Is he ever-living, is he beautiful, have many fostered his sons? Are his daughters dear and beautiful in the eyes of the men of the earth? Is he in the sky or in the earth, or in the water, in rivers, in mountains, in valleys? Give us an account of him: how shall he be seen, how is he loved, how is he found, is he found in youth, in old age.

The girl's speech is very much a literary one; the Latin words show an interest in cadences and rhyme but as a seventh-century man's imaginative account of what a pagan might have said, it gives us real insights into the world of pre-Norman Ireland.

All this is, however, straying far from the fifth century. One solution to the problem of the 'real fifth-century facts' is to rely not so much on the documentary record, which, as we have seen, is controversial, but rather on archaeology. My first piece of evidence in this regard is a hoard of silver ingots, of Roman type, found in Balline in Co Limerick. One of these ingots comes from the workshop of a man named ISAS which the influential Roman historian F. J. Haverfield pointed out in 1900 was the

Latin form of the Jewish name Isaac (Collingwood & Wright 1990, 31). Isaac had a problem with his stamp-maker, the man who produced the tool which marked the ingots as his. When creating the stamp, the man produced a stamp in which the first S of Isas is reversed or written backwards. Ingots, bearing Isas' name and with exactly this same mistake have also been found in Kent, one on the legionary fort at Richborough and another on the beach near Reculver. There is nothing to date these ingots but it seems reasonable to assume they date to a period either before or not very long after the Roman withdrawal from Britain, in the early years of the fifth century AD. Here, then, we have a real fifth-century fact: a man with a Jewish name was producing silver ingots which ended up in both Kent and Limerick. The Christian significance of the find is reinforced by the presence, on another of the Balline ingots, of the *chi-rho* monogram, the sign which the early church connected with the conversion of the Emperor Constantine at the Milvian bridge.

A second 'fifth-century fact' concerns Irish ogam stones, pillars of stone, inscribed in a uniquely Irish alphabet with the names of individuals. These have traditionally been viewed by archaeologists as undatable except within very broad limits; we have no excavated example in its original context and there is nothing organic about a piece of stone which allows us to use our modern scientific dating techniques of carbon-fourteen dating or dendrochronology. On linguistic grounds, however, we can say that the name forms go through a variety of changes; just as Latin develops into the modern Romance languages of French, Italian and Spanish, so Irish moves from Primitive to modern Irish. The early stages in this linguistic progression can be seen on the ogam stones and linguists have identified the first recognisable stage, known as pre-apocope stones, as fifth-century in date.

When ogam stones are analysed in this way, it becomes apparent that the majority are of either fifth or sixth century date. More interestingly for our purposes, we begin to see that amongst the stones showing fifth-century styles, we find a num-

ber where the men being commemorated have Latin names: a
son of Marianus at Rathglass in Co Carlow and another
Marianus in Co Kerry as well as a man called Sagittarius or
archer in Co Cork. Of sixth-century type we have a son of
Marinus the sailor, another called Vitalinus in Co Kerry and a
man named Amatus in Ardmore, Co Waterford. This last bears a
name commonly found amongst early Christians but the possibility exists that some of the fifth-century stones also commemo-
rate Christians – the stone of Marianus, from Co Kerry, for example, has an extremely elaborate cross on its front face.

In addition to the fifth-century style ogam stones that show
individuals with Latin names, we also have fifth-century style
ogam stones which apparently give an Irish version of the HIC
IACET burial formula, found commonly on Christian memorials
on the Continent and occasionally in Britain. The Irish version
uses the word KOI, which is apparently a Primitive Irish word
meaning 'Here'. Some of these KOI stones show characteristics
of the fifth-century style and their Christian significance is enhanced by the presence of a cross on the front face of the stone.

Interestingly, there are a number of fifth-century ogam
stones with crosses and/or inscribed with the KOI formula from
the Dingle peninsula. The late Dr Thomas Fanning excavated an
early ecclesiastical site from this area at Reask where he found
but discounted a fourth-century C14 date for the earliest material
on the site; he remarked that there was no reason to assume
Christianity had been present in the area as early as the fifth
century (Fanning 1981, 113-15, 121). I would argue that the presence of Christian ogam stones of fifth-century date in the immediate vicinity requires us to take that C14 date more seriously.

The second fifth-century fact, therefore, is that we have evidence for fifth-century Irish Christians commemorated on a number of ogam stones from the southern half of the country. Some
of these Christians had Latin names and they used an Irish form
of a burial formula common in the fifth-century Roman world.
We do not know, unfortunately, whether there were Christians
in the north of the country at the same time – most ogam stones

tend to be found in the south and all we can say so far is that
there is no evidence of early Christian inscriptions on the relatively few stones found north of the Dublin/Galway line.

A third fifth-century fact is based on a stone found in the
early Christian cemetery of St Mattias in Trier, on the western
German border close to Luxembourg. This is the so-called
Scottus stone and it reads: 'Here happily lies Scottus, who lived
65 years. His wife, Dulcis, erected this gravestone out of love.
Oh Scottus, peace be with you.' The final prayer is obviously
Christian and this is reinforced by the two doves at the bottom
of the slab. The stone was dated to the fifth century by analogy
with the handwriting on other graveslabs in the vicinity. Some
of these slabs also include dating formulae in their inscriptions,
which allows us to date the sequence of handwriting styles. The
word *Scottus*, plural *Scotti* is, of course well known and there is
some debate whether it is limited to Irishmen or whether it can
be used to also refer to Scots – it is certainly used by Orosius to
refer to inhabitants of the Isle of Man at the beginning of the fifth
century AD. As a minimum, therefore, it would appear to refer
to speakers of a Gaelic language. Thus, in Trier, we have the
gravestone erected to the memory of a fifth-century Christian
whose name implies that he was a speaker of Primitive Irish.

Bearing these three fifth-century facts in mind, (1) that silver
ingots produced in a Christian milieu could end up both in Co
Limerick and in Kent; (2) that fifth-century Christians, some
with Latin names, are commemorated on ogam stones from
southern Ireland and (3) that a Christian Irish-speaker was
buried in a fifth-century graveyard in the Roman city of Trier,
one can turn to the documentary sources. Immediately, one
notes that just as with the archaeological material, we have two
identifiable sources for Irish Christianity, one deriving from
Pope Celestine and his emissary, Palladius; the other, the writings of the Romanised Briton, Patrick. As with our three facts,
we see evidence of both continental and British influence, both
arising out of the broader context of late Roman civilisation.
That civilisation varied geographically as well as chronologically

– and in Britain, on Rome's most northerly as well as its most western frontier, the impact of imperial administration was at its lightest. It has often been noted that in the opening words of his *Confessio*, Patrick claims that his father and grandfather were both Christian clerics, that they owned a small villa and that, as he points out in his *Letter to Coroticus*, his father was a decurion, reinforcing the notion that he came from a relatively wealthy family which enjoyed many of the trappings of middle-class Roman culture. What has not, I think, been said before, is that identifying your father and your grandfather in this way is a particularly Celtic custom; Roman name-forms are not normally structured in this three-generational fashion. In other words, Patrick's background may have been influenced by Roman culture but he was also strongly marked by the conventions of the Celtic civilisations around the Irish Sea.

In this context, it is interesting to note Patrick's words about the people he had converted to Christ: they had, he says, the somewhat irritating habit of trying to put jewellery on his altar and they could not understand why he did not want them. This makes perfect sense in the cultural world of Romanised Britain. We have now excavated a number of Roman temples in Britain, some dedicated to gods with both Roman and Celtic names, and one of the features of these temples is the amount of jewellery and coins which have been placed as votive offerings within the shrine.

Patrick, however, says this was a habit not of his British kinsmen but rather of the Irish converts to Christianity whom he met in Ireland. It is not a habit which we can identify in Iron Age Ireland; the only Irish examples of such a custom is the existence of Roman coins buried around the entrance of Newgrange and a single Roman coin from the site of the great henge complex at the Giant's Ring, outside Belfast. Such coins were obviously imports and, indeed, the custom of burying them at these sites appears also to be an imported one. In short, if the Irish men and women whom Patrick encountered were in the habit of throwing jewellery at his altar, they were doing so because they had acquired this way of worship from pagan Roman Britain.

But who were these men and women? Many scholars have emphasised the possibility that he converted slaves, possibly fellow Britons captured by Irish raiders. One might also stress the passage in the *Confessio* in which the saint states that he had converted the sons and daughters of Irish kings together with a blessed Irish woman, born noble. Patrick also writes that he used to travel about with a retinue composed of kings' sons and that he used to give presents to their royal fathers in order to be allowed to conduct his missionary work. When he was captured on one occasion, apparently by some of these royal dynasts, he and his companions had sufficiently powerful friends to persuade his captors to let him free. In other words, Patrick's Irish mission operated within a high-status world of Irish nobility, in keeping with the provincial nobility of his family background in Britain. My suggestion is that we should identify those Irish nobles more specifically, as people who had already been Romanised to the point where they had adopted a number of the social customs of Roman Britain. Just as the earliest evidence for Irish Christianity is clearly derivative of the wider Roman world, so too, I would argue, Christianity in Ireland was most likely to have been accepted by those who already favoured the Roman way of life.

This identification of the social class and political instincts of Patrick's likely converts can also help to explain the original choice of Armagh as a centre of Patrick's cult. It is important to say 'a' centre rather than 'the' centre; the first detailed evidence that we have of Patrick's cult, in the later seventh century AD, does not, in fact, specify that Armagh was anything more than one of a number of churches in Ireland that claimed a special connection with the saint. The process through which the argument first for Patrick's primacy within Ireland and secondly for the settlement of Armagh as the seat of a national archbishopric was a long one; indeed, it was still being argued over in the twelfth century as the Normans arrived and continued to be a matter for debate throughout the history of the medieval colony. The details of that debate is a subject for another lecture and another occasion; the purpose here is to outline the possible fifth-century reasons why a Christian cult centre, dedicated to Patrick's church, might have been established at Armagh in the first place.

It has often been suggested that Patrick chose Armagh because it was associated with a provincial kingdom of Ulster; the kingdom of Conchobar mac Nessa, his heroic nephew Cú Chulainn and the other so-called Knights of the Red Branch, men whose mythic exploits were renowned in medieval Irish legend. These suggestions were apparently strengthened by the results of the important excavations by Dudley Waterman at Navan fort, some miles outside Armagh city. These excavations, now published by Dr Chris Lynn, have produced a complex of prehistoric monuments including an Iron Age temple – the so-called Forty-Metre structure. The fortunate survival of the stump of the central post in this structure give us a felling date of 95 BC. Thus we have a major ritual centre at almost exactly the same date at which our medieval authors believed Cú Chulainn lived.

The problem with this interpretation in that these legends are all much later in date than the fifth century AD whilst the Forty-Metre structure is not only some distance from the church centre of Armagh itself but is also almost five hundred years too early. Tying the arrival of Patrick to this putative kingdom is akin to the difficulties about Patrician traditions in general; it is using non-fifth-century material to explain fifth-century events.

Instead, the answer may lie in the sculpture which was found in the foundations of the Protestant Cathedral of Armagh, when that was being rebuilt in the 1840s. The context of that sculpture is provided by excavations on Cathedral Hill in the 1960s and later, which showed that the cathedral was located within a massive pre-existing enclosure encircling the hill, and in the surrounding area. Twigs and branches from within the enclosure ditch give us C14 dates, with 95% probability of accuracy, to the period 130-600 AD. This enclosure was therefore in working use on the hill of Armagh in the fifth century.

The sculpture from within the site is varied. Perhaps most famous are the three animals known as the Armagh bears – only two of these unfortunately now survive. In Irish archaeology these are described as Celtic but they are Celtic only in the way that much of provincial Roman sculpture north of the Alps is Celtic; the sculptor has clearly been heavily influenced by the naturalistic styles originating in the Mediterranean. The closest parallels identified for them come from Senlis and Limoges in Roman Gaul. There are also a number of heads, at least some of which appear to belong to Romano-Celtic tradition of isolated stone heads, which we find attested from Provence to Donegal.

In addition, there is a small squat figure, described in 1974 by the Scottish expert, Dr Anne Ross, as being 'more at home in northern Britain than in northern Ireland', with his hair splaying out around his head in the manner of fourth-century Roman depictions of the *Sol Invicta* or the unconquered sun (Ross 1967, 477). She cites a parallel figure at Maryport; there are also similar statues from south-west England. Finally, there is the figure now on show in the Cathedral but originally from the townland of Tanderagee; a photograph of a similar figure, known as the 'Lurgan figure' is on show in the Armagh county museum. There is also a parallel figure from Roman Dijon in Burgundy and I have identified another in Scotland.

Statues of both humans and animals are a feature of Roman temples in both Britain and the Continent; it seems quite clear that the evidence from Cathedral Hill indicates the presence of a temple complex of Roman type. The presence of the *Sol Invicta* figure indicates that such a temple is likely to have been in existence in the fourth and fifth centuries when the cult of the Unconquered Sun was at its height – such a date coincides with the indications of the C14 dates from the surrounding enclosure ditch.

The literary account of the questions posed by the king of Tara's daughters to Patrick include the questions who is God, where is God and, most crucially, whose God is he? In recent years a number of Celtic scholars have been debating the possible pre-Christian significance of a phrase which occurs in a number of Irish saga texts: *tongu día tonges mo thúath*, 'I swear by the God by whom my people swear'. We do not know exactly where Patrick or indeed, his Continental counterpart, Palladius operated in Ireland but we have seen that the first evidence for Christianity in Ireland indicates that they included Irishmen who had translated Roman Christian burial formulae into their own vernacular as well as others, who used conventional Roman graveslabs when buried in Roman cities abroad. In Patrick's own writings we see that his mission resulted in converts among the native ruling class and ones who had adopted the cultural habits of Roman Britons worshipping at pagan temples. At Cathedral Hill, we see what is apparently a temple site of Romano-British type on the hill which later became the centre of the great ecclesiastical settlement of Armagh. The answer for the king of Tara's daughter is that Patrick's God was the Christian God, firmly ensconced as the sole religious cult in the fifth-century Roman world. He was the God who had been worshiped over three generations by Patrick's high-status British relatives and as a consequence of the fifth-century missions he became the God of those fifth-century Irish families who had already adopted Roman ways.

Bibliography

Collingwood R. G. & Wright, R. P., *The Roman Inscriptions of Britain* Vol II, fascicule 1, Alan Sutton Publishing Ltd, Gloucester 1990

Fanning, T. 'Excavation of an early Christian cemetery and settlement at Reask, Co Kerry', *Proceedings of the Royal Irish Academy* 81C, 1981, 67-172

Lynn, C. J., *Excavations at Navan Fort 1961-71 by D. M. Waterman*, HMSO, Belfast 1997

Ross, Anne, *Pagan Celtic Britain*, Routledge & Keegan, London 1967.

Swift, Catherine, *Ogam Stones and the earliest Irish Christians*, Maynooth Monographs, series minor 2, Maynooth 1996

— 'The gods of Newgrange and Romano-Celtic tradition' in G. Burenhult & S. Westergaard, eds., *Stones and Bones: Formal Disposal of the Dead in Atlantic Europe*, BAR International series 1201, Oxford 2003, pp.53-63

This lecture was originally delivered under the title 'Patrician and non-Patrician mission to Ireland and the establishment of Armagh' on 23 October 2001.

The Christianisation of the Dublin Vikings

Howard B. Clarke

From a standard western European perspective, there are dangers in the manner in which we might perceive a subject of this kind. One danger lies in our perception of Christianity itself. In order to understand how pagans of the Viking Age may have reacted to pressures to convert, we have to cast aside all of the developments that occurred in the second millennium AD, such as the papal reform movement of the late eleventh century, the Reformation and Counter-Reformation of the sixteenth century, the doctrine of papal infallibility established in the late nineteenth century, or Vatican II in the late twentieth century. Instead we have to travel back in time to a world, in Ireland, where the *célí Dé* reform movement was in progress (and focused to a significant degree on churches at Finglas and Tallaght), where clerical celibacy was hardly enforced, where the prohibited degrees of marriage were either uncertain or ignored, and where the payment of tithes to support parish priests had not been regularised. In other words, 'Christianity' would not have meant then what it may mean now.

The second danger is that of taking a christocentric view of paganism as a matter of course. This is usually the case whenever scholars from the core areas of Latin Christendom consider the question of conversion of pagans. The ultimate 'victory' of Christianity over paganism tends to be presumed as inevitable and entirely justified; the process is seen from a Christian perspective, just as the Vikings themselves (in Ireland) are seen from a native perspective. Paganism is one aspect of the otherness of these strangers to our shores, together with their language. Only from the Old Norse poetry and later sagas do we

derive any feeling for the other side. Implicit in this christocentric viewpoint is a belief in the innate superiority of a theistic religious system over a polytheistic one. Down through the ages,
acceptance of the 'one true God' has been accompanied by a
sense of triumphalism over more primitive forms of religious
belief. As has been pointed out, intolerance of alternative sys-
tems of belief may well have been viewed by Scandinavian
pagans as a distinctly unattractive feature of Christianity and
one reason why the conversion process in the homelands took
so many generations to complete.[1] The same may well have
been true of Ireland. Indeed, so blind has been this intolerance
that many Christians fail to comprehend that their own system
is, from a socio-anthropological standpoint, deeply polytheistic
– the cult of many saints taking the place of the cult of many
gods. It is best, therefore, to consider the subject of the christian-
isation of the Dublin Vikings from a socio-anthropological perspective, putting aside more narrowly theological aspects and
prejudices.

   If we ask ourselves how and when did the Dublin Vikings accept Christianity *en masse*, the short answer is that we do not
know because nobody tells us. Even the foundation of the first
cathedral went unrecorded in the annals, though King Sitriuc (=
Sigtryggr) Silkbeard's pilgrimage to Rome in 1028 is documented.[2] One of the consequences of the former event is that the
foundation date of Christ Church Cathedral is, to this day, still
misrepresented on the official notice-board inside the entrance
gate. The traditional date 1038 is a late medieval error, for Sitriuc
had been deposed as king two years earlier;[3] accordingly a date
shortly after his return from Italy is the best estimate that can be
made. Only around this time, c. 1030, was a bishop (Dúnán) installed, implying that a critical mass of Christian adherents existed in the town and opening up the possibility that other
priests might be consecrated for the local population, that individual parishes might be formed, and that the people might at
last be able to listen to the occasional sermon. By c. 1030, however,
the people of Dublin and its immediate hinterland should not be

thought of as Vikings. Since the 980s, in the aftermath of their
overwhelming defeat by Máel Sechnaill II's forces at the battle of
Tara,[4] the Dubliners had been progressively reduced politically,
whilst at the same time maintaining a healthy disrespect for
those in authority, as we see more famously at the battle of
Clontarf (1014). This was a role they would play right down to
1171, when the last Norse king was defeated and executed by
the Anglo-French invaders.[5] The decisive conversion, therefore,
was more of an Hiberno-Norse occurrence than a specifically
Viking one, a point that illustrates the need to ask the right questions in the first place before attempting to answer them.

We need also to be aware of similar processes elsewhere in
the Viking world, both in the Scandinavian homelands
(Denmark, Norway and Sweden) and in other colonial contexts,
such as north-eastern England, Iceland, Normandy and the
Scottish islands. This is a big subject, but I propose to look
briefly at one of the best documented of these, Denmark, which
for their Frankish neighbours was a source of considerable
fascination and an entry-point for a few brave missionaries. At a
remarkably early date, in 826, its king, Harald Klak, accepted
Christianity at Ingelheim, the western emperor, Louis the Pious,
presiding over the proceedings.[6] This led a few years later to the
first Christian mission to Scandinavia of St Ansgar, which ultimately failed. Mid-ninth-century Frankish sources record a fairly
consistent effort to persuade individual Danes to convert, but
there was no mass conversion at all.[7] In 864 Pope Nicholas I
wrote to King Horic II to thank him for sending alms to Rome
and to reprimand him for continuing to worship idols.[8]
Ambivalence of this kind has a long history in this context.
Ambassadors from Denmark sometimes accepted baptism in
Frankia, but did not practise Christianity when they went back
home.[9] Indeed, to have done so would have been difficult, for
there were virtually no churches or priests and no bishops. A
church is known to have been established at Hedeby (Haithabu)
for the Danish and Saxon traders who frequented it, but its pre-
cise location has not yet been identified archaeologically.[10]

Accordingly we should not draw too hard and fast a distinction between Christian Franks and pagan Danes. In this period a 'Christian' in this part of the world was anyone who had undergone the ceremony of *prima signatio* or actual baptism. It seems clear that such rituals were not always properly understood by pagans. When missionaries went to Birka, another trading settlement in Sweden, in the mid-ninth century, they were confronted by temples and regular sacrifices, and probably learnt to work alongside accepted social norms in order to make any progress at all.[11] To all appearances very little progress was in fact made, with the result that, when the Danish Great Army landed in eastern England in 865 and began its campaign of material and political destruction, it was regarded by the Christian Anglo-Saxons as an entirely heathen body. The biographer of King Alfred of Wessex, the Welsh priest Asser, presents the Viking wars as a series of Christian defeats by pagans and victories over pagans.[12] Alfred's own perspective was probably not so very different; when he was fortunate enough to defeat Guthrum at the battle of Edington in 878, a mark of triumph was to arrange with great ceremony the baptism of his adversary and thirty of his leading followers.[13] Guthrum comes across rather like some of the Danish rulers themselves: prepared to be well-disposed towards Christianity, yet quite incapable of bringing along with him the great majority of his people.

The failure of Christianity to make decisive inroads into hearts and minds in Denmark is reflected in the fascinating description of Hedeby c. 950 by a relatively impartial observer, the Arab visitor, Al-Tartushi. The Christian church was still there, but the mass of the population was still thoroughly pagan:

Its people worship Sirius except for a few who are Christians and have a church there. A feast is held to honour their deity and to eat and drink. Any man who slaughters a sacrificial animal – whether it is an ox, ram, goat, or pig – fastens it up on poles outside the door of his house to show that he has made his sacrifice in honour of the god.[14]

Archaeologists have found animal masks in the harbour area

of Hedeby, perhaps part of a pagan cult of some kind.[15] Only in the next generation would a king of Denmark, Harald Bluetooth, claim on the great runic stone at Jelling in central Jutland that he had made all the Danes Christian.[16] He himself was converted c. 965, but the breadth of his claim is to be doubted. His son, Sven Forkbeard, revolted against his father as part of a pagan reaction, though he was remembered later as a founder of churches.[17] Mass conversion, if it came at all, occurred in the next reign, that of Knutr the Great, who became king of England in 1016 and of Denmark in 1019. In 1027 Knutr made a formal visit to Rome,[18] an act that was apparently emulated by Sitriuc of Dublin in the following year. As elsewhere in the Scandinavian world, Christianity had become almost fashionable and to that extent more generally acceptable to large numbers of people. Even so, the whole of Denmark was not divided up into dioceses until c. 1060, when there were still no individual parishes and no support-system for priests in the form of tithes.[19] There can be no doubt that the conversion of the Danes from paganism to Christianity was an exceedingly hesitant and long-drawnout process.

Turning back now to Dublin, we may be better prepared to interpret such evidence as we have. Relevant 'events' before c. 1030 are few and far between, as recorded in the native written sources. With one exception (which I shall mention towards the end), the first relevant event was of course the initial settlement of 841.[20] This must have been traumatic enough for local Christians and it is quite possible that the Vikings took over the monastic site of Duiblinn, as they did that at Annagassan further north.[21] Recent finds of pagan burials between the pool in the River Poddle and the presumed site of the monastery at Dublin may belong to this early phase of Viking activity.[22] The pagan graves discovered long ago at Kilmainham and Islandbridge have normally been associated with the *longphort* phase of settlement, which lasted down to 902.[23] Towards the end of this period, across the water in England, a Danish king of York, Guthfrith, was accorded a Christian burial in the cathedral there in 895,[24] making him another example of a high-status convert. Dublin was recaptured by Vikings in 917 and raiding resumed in its hinterland in particular.[25] The spring raid of 929 was conducted with an exquisite sense of place and timing, on Kildare on St Brigid's Day,[26] when the monastery would have been full of pilgrims; clearly the Vikings were aware of the Christian calendar, but only for the purposes of pagan profit. The last great raid out of Dublin occurred in 951, to Kells and its district, when cattle, horses, gold, silver and the menfolk were taken away.[27]

By the third quarter of the tenth century, there appears to have been a change of perception on the part of the Irish annalists: the Scandinavians cease to be referred to as heathens or Gentiles.[28] In 943 the future king of Dublin, Amlaíb (= Óláfr) Cúarán, received baptism over in England, though probably (like the Danish Guthrum before) as a mark of political submission.[29] He subsequently married two Irish women and may have been at least tolerant of Christianity. Following his defeat at Tara, he retired to Iona,[30] a monastery that had suffered so grievously at the hands of Vikings in the past. Yet we still have no clear evidence for regular Christian observance at Dublin, apart from the earliest burials discovered on the sites of the churches of St Bridget and St Michael le Pole (as it was later known).[31] If these are indeed to be interpreted as evidence of a Christian presence at Dublin by the second half of the tenth century, it should be noted that these sites lay outside the main defensive enclosure.[32] The prevailing culture inside may still have been pagan, as is suggested by another recorded event in 995. When Máel Sechnaill II captured the town (for the third time) in that year, he took away two prized possessions, one of which was the ring of Thor.[33] If this was a heavy, oath-swearing ring of Scandinavian type, pagan observances may still have mattered to at least some of the leading men. Furthermore, when Sitriuc Silkbeard was recruiting abroad in the winter of 1013-14 for warriors to oppose Brian Bóruma, he apparently had no qualms about including pagans among them.[34] Only towards the end of his long life did he make his decisive gesture in favour of

Christianity. Even then, the initial endowment of Christ Church was not particularly generous, amounting to a site for the building, land at Grangegorman, and some gold and silver.[35] The more extensive estate of the cathedral detailed in *Alen's Register* seems to date from the twelfth century rather than the eleventh.[36] From 1052 onwards, Dublin was usually overlorded by one or other of the native provincial kings and there was a trickle of patronage in the form of land from some of them as well as from local landowners.

In addition to these occasional documentary clues, we have a certain amount of archaeological evidence. Altogether an estimated eighty to ninety pagan Viking graves are known from the immediate Dublin area.[37] About 10% are those of females, who presumably came either directly from Norway or from pagan Scandinavian communities in the Scottish Isles. Most of these graves were discovered in the nineteenth century and were not scientifically excavated;[38] our understanding of them may increase when they have been published as fully as is now possible in a forthcoming volume. An important archaeological discovery of recent times is a number of Patrick Wallace's Type 1 houses at Essex Street West dating from the second half of the ninth century.[39] Their construction is not typically Scandinavian and they have been interpreted as evidence of cultural interaction between the local Irish and the newcomers at an early stage. In addition there are signs of pagan burial rites in the form of cattle heads buried with humans and the tops of two human skulls.[40] A similar piece of skull found at Ribe in western Jutland was embellished with a runic inscription![41] The number of pagan burials is by far the largest concentration in Ireland, yet not very impressive for a period of about sixty years (841-902). Some of the Viking dead may have been cremated, as in the homelands; others may not have been buried in accordance with pagan ritual; still others, of course (perhaps the majority), have never been found at all. An absence of pagan burials in tenth-century levels should not necessarily be explained by an absence of pagan beliefs. After c. 950 pagan burials tend to disappear from coastal districts of Norway, but not from further inland.[42] A number of factors may have been at work and the archaeological prospects have long been compromised by the continuous history of urban build-up at Dublin since the Viking Age.

Scandinavian cultural artefacts of many different types are well attested in the archaeology of Dublin right down to the twelfth century. The remains of ships and boats reflect the mainstream Scandinavian tradition; the Dublin fleet was still a major asset in the mid-twelfth century, a fact that is best illustrated by its use in King Henry II's expedition to Wales in 1165.[43] A warship (known as Skuldelev 2) built of oak from eastern Ireland in 1060, very possibly at Dublin, has turned up as a deliberately scuttled shipwreck in Roskilde Fjord in Denmark.[44] Graffiti and models of ships are also in conformity with this evidence in that they seem to represent vessels of Nordic type.[45] The decorated wood is a mixture of native and Scandinavian styles, especially Norwegian Ringerike.[46] Five of these objects have been classified as crooks and could conceivably have been used in an ecclesiastical milieu.[47] About a dozen runic inscriptions have been found etched on pieces of wood, with a general dating range of 950-1125.[48] These brief texts indicate that both West and East Scandinavian speech would have been heard in Dublin, that is, there were Norwegians and Danes in the population.[49] Donnchadh Ó Corráin has suggested that the lost *Brjáns Saga* was written in Norse, in Dublin, c. 1100;[50] as in the northern Danelaw of England, Norse speech may have survived in Dublin into the twelfth century.[51] It would have been perfectly natural, therefore, to refer to the Hiberno-Norse population by the Icelandic usage, Ostmen ('men from the east').

These pagan and Scandinavian cultural manifestations have their Christian and Irish counterparts. In a sophisticated argument, Charles Doherty has suggested that Columban missionaries may have been seeking converts in tenth-century Dublin.[52] More tangible is the evidence from two other cemeteries near Dublin, one north and the other south of the Liffey. That at Castleknock contained an estimated 1,200 graves, about a third of which were excavated archaeologically in 1938. Their estimated dating range is from the mid-ninth to the mid-eleventh century,[53] that is, the Viking Age and well beyond it. The cemetery uncovered more recently at Cabinteely (not far from a place whose name implies Scandinavian settlement – Loughlinstown) contained over 1,500 skeletons extending from the late fifth to the late twelfth century.[54] In both cases, therefore, regular, organised, Christian burial practices were being maintained coincidentally with the Viking settlement; Christian communities 8 km and 12.5 km from Dublin must have become quite accustomed to living alongside pagan ones. One important detail from the Castleknock analysis is that, where the sex of the skeletons could be determined, 42% were female.[55] This in turn brings to mind one other significant 'event' recorded in the annals. It took place at Howth in the year 821, in the form of one of the earliest recorded Viking raids in the Dublin district. These particular Vikings were choosy: they stole, not cattle or horses or gold or silver, but according to the *Annals of Ulster* 'a great number of women'![56]

By bringing women into the picture, we may at last have part of an answer to the question of how and when the Dublin Vikings were christianised. As we know from an excellent survey of the Norwegian evidence, the earliest Viking raiders in Ireland took back to Norway significant quantities of Insular loot.[57] Some of this was refashioned there into jewellery and ornaments, suggesting that one of the motives behind these raids was to please the womenfolk back home.[58] From the year 837, however, the Vikings showed greater commitment to the establishment of permanent bases in Ireland. Again they brought relatively few women with them, hence the low ratio at Kilmainham and Islandbridge. Ireland was different from the Northern and Western Isles of Scotland; it was full of kings and their armies, and very dangerous from a Norwegian perspective, as well as being farther from home. The incident recorded in 821 may hint at what would become commonplace, that most Vikings operating in Ireland liaised one way or another with native women. The same seems to have happened in Normandy later on.[59] Some native women became wives, others concubines, and still others slaves. The territory controlled by the Dublin Vikings was initially small. It was full of native Irish, men and women, as the cemeteries at Castleknock and Cabinteely (and no doubt elsewhere) have demonstrated. It is possible that some of the dead there were Scandinavians, accorded Christian burial by their Christian wives and relatives. Most of the ordinary churches would have been small, with little or nothing of value from a Viking perspective. They may well have continued in use wherever there was a native population. Accordingly pagan burial rites died out earlier than pagan beliefs and observances. Most Dublin Vikings probably continued to believe in the efficacy of Odin as the god of war and of Thor as the god of natural forces. They would have had the mentality of the tenth-century saga character, Helgi the Lean, who was nominally a Christian but who reverted to Thor when in a rough sea or in big trouble.[60]

Amlaíb Cúarán, king of Dublin from 945 to 980, made two attempts to rule at York.[61] There the Christian church had continued to survive, though Archbishop Wulfstan I in particular acquired a dubious reputation as a collaborator with the pagan Danes.[62] In such an environment, compromises must have been made by both Christians and pagans. One is reminded of the comment of the German chronicler, Widukind, in 968: 'The Danes had long been Christians but they nevertheless worshipped idols with pagan rituals.'[63] One is reminded, too, of the compromise reached in Iceland when the national assembly opted for Christianity in 999 or 1000: pagans would be permitted, at least for a while, to eat horse flesh, to indulge in animal sacrifices in private, and to practise infant exposure.[64] In the territory of the Dublin Hiberno-Norsemen, the Rathdown graveslabs reflect a mixed culture of this kind.[65] The churches of St Bridget and St Michael (le Pole), situated outside the main settlement, may represent the way in which Christian adherents began to establish themselves, on the margins.

Only later, as we have seen, did an Hiberno-Norse king see fit to set up a major Christian presence inside the defences, headed by a bishop. As an old man, Sitriuc Silkbeard may have decided to opt publicly for his mother's faith. As Peter Sawyer has commented, 'to establish a permanent ecclesiastical presence ... missionaries needed the commitment of Scandinavian rulers, not merely tolerance'.[66] By c. 1030 Christianity had probably been tolerated in and around Dublin for a long time, but it had not been accorded official recognition. And when official recognition did come from inside the community, it was withheld from outside. At the synod of Ráith Bressail in 1111, the diocese of Dublin was subsumed into the native diocese of Glendalough;[67] apart from anything else, Dublin's allegiance to Canterbury in England made it suspect, or at least different. Only at the later synod of 1152 was it accepted and, for political reasons, accorded metropolitan status.[68] Even so, elements of paganism, native Irish as well as Scandinavian, continued to exist as a kind of sub-culture. Doubting readers are invited to recall how many times, in an ostensibly Christian celebration, they have sacrificed a turkey or other animal at the winter solstice and have eaten its flesh; they have decorated a typically Nordic tree with baubles and figurines of mythical and semi-mythical beings; they have played games and sung songs with their relatives and friends; and they have consumed far more food and alcoholic drink than is good for them. Pagan Vikings at Dublin would have understood perfectly!

References
1. Sawyer, Peter, 'The process of Scandinavian christianization in the tenth and eleventh centuries' in Sawyer, Birgit, Sawyer, Peter and Wood, Ian, ed., *The Christianization of Scandinavia*, Viktoria Bokförlag, Alingsås 1987, p. 84.
2. *AU*, pp. 466-7.
3. *Ann. Tig.*, Vol 2, p. 268; Gwynn, Aubrey, 'The origins of the See of Dublin' in *The Irish Church in the Eleventh and Twelfth Centuries*, ed. Gerard O'Brien, Four Courts Press, Blackrock 1992, pp. 50-67.
4. *AU*, pp. 414-15.
5. Scott, A. B. and Martin, F. X., ed., *Expugnatio Hibernica: the Conquest of Ireland by Giraldus Cambrensis*, Royal Irish Academy, Dublin 1978, pp. 76-9.

6. Wood, Ian, 'Christians and pagans in ninth-century Scandinavia' in Sawyer, Birgit, Sawyer, Peter and Wood, Ian, ed., *The Christianization of Scandinavia*, Viktoria Bokförlag, Alingsås 1987, pp. 36-7.

7. ibid., pp. 36-67.

8. ibid., p. 49.

9. ibid., p. 50.

10. ibid., p. 51.

11. ibid., pp. 53-4, 74-5.

12. Keynes, Simon and Lapidge, Michael, trans., *Alfred the Great: Asser's 'Life of King Alfred' and Other Contemporary Sources*, Penguin Books, Harmondsworth 1983, pp. 68, 69, 74, 76-81, 83-5, 87.

13. ibid., p. 85; Whitelock, Dorothy, with Douglas, D. C. and Tucker, S. I., trans., *The Anglo-Saxon Chronicle: a Revised Translation*, Eyre and Spottiswoode, London 1961, pp. 49-50.

14. Quoted in Brøndsted, Johannes, *The Vikings*, Penguin Books, Harmondsworth 1965, p. 42.

15. Wood, 'Christians and pagans', p. 65.

16. Sawyer, 'Process of Scandinavian christianization', p. 70.

17. ibid., pp. 80-1.

18. Lawson, M. K., *Cnut: the Danes in England in the Early Eleventh Century*, Longman, London and New York 1993, pp. 158-9 and passim.

19. Sawyer, 'Process of Scandinavian christianization', pp. 78-9, 83.

20. *AU*, pp. 298-9.

21. Clarke, H. B., 'Proto-towns and towns in Ireland and Britain in the ninth and tenth centuries' in Clarke, H. B., Ní Mhaonaigh, Máire and Ó Floinn, Raghnall, ed., *Ireland and Scandinavia in the Early Viking Age*, Four Courts Press, Dublin 1998, p. 348; Ó Floinn, Raghnall, 'The archaeology of the Early Viking Age in Ireland' in Clarke, H. B., Ní Mhaonaigh, Máire and Ó Floinn, Raghnall, ed., *Ireland and Scandinavia in the Early Viking Age*, Four Courts Press, Dublin 1998, p. 162.

22. Simpson, Linzi, 'Ninth-century Viking burials in Dublin', *Archaeology Ireland* XVII/3 (autumn 2003), p. 5.

23. O'Brien, Elizabeth, 'The location and context of Viking burials at Kilmainham and Islandbridge, Dublin' in Clarke, H. B., Ní Mhaonaigh, Máire and Ó Floinn, Raghnall, ed., *Ireland and Scandinavia in the Early Viking Age*, Four Courts Press, Dublin 1998, pp. 203-21.

24. Campbell, Alistair, ed., *The Chronicle of Æthelweard*, Nelson, London 1962, p. 51.

25. *AU*, pp. 366-7; Clarke, H. B., 'The bloodied eagle: the Vikings and the development of Dublin, 841-1014', *The Irish Sword* XVIII/71 (summer 1991), pp. 102-5 and fig. 2.

26. *AFM*, Vol 2, pp. 622-3.

27. *AU*, pp. 396-7.

28. Abrams, Lesley, 'The conversion of the Scandinavians of Dublin', *Anglo-Norman Studies* XX (1997), pp. 9-13.

29. ibid., pp. 23-5; Whitelock, Douglas and Tucker, *Anglo-Saxon Chronicle*, p. 71.

30. *Chron. Scot.*, pp. 226-7; *AFM*, Vol 2, pp. 710-13.

31. Gowen, Margaret, 'Excavations at the site of the church and tower of St Michael le Pole, Dublin' in Duffy, Seán, ed., *Medieval Dublin II: Proceedings of the Friends of Medieval Dublin Symposium 2000*, Four Courts Press, Dublin 2001, pp. 26, 34-7, 41, 48-9 and figs 11, 12; plates 1-3.

32. Clarke, H. B., 'Conversion, church and cathedral: the Diocese of Dublin to 1152' in Kelly, James and Keogh, Dáire, ed., *History of the Catholic Diocese of Dublin*, Four Courts Press, Dublin 2000, fig. 6.

33. *Chron. Scot.*, pp. 234-5; *AFM*, Vol 2, pp. 732-3.

34. Ryan, John, 'The Battle of Clontarf', *Journal of the Royal Society of Antiquaries of Ireland* LXVIII (1938), pp. 15-17.

35. McNeill, Charles, ed., *Calendar of Archbishop Alen's Register c. 1172-1534*, Royal Society of Antiquaries of Ireland, Dublin 1950, p. 28.

36. ibid., pp. 28-9; Clarke, 'Conversion, church and cathedral', pp. 35-6 and fig. 3.

37. Ó Floinn, 'Archaeology of the Early Viking Age', p. 142.

38. O'Brien, 'Location and context of Viking burials', pp. 206-11 and fig. 7.3.

39. Simpson, Linzi, *Director's Findings: Temple Bar West*, Temple Bar Properties, Dublin 1999, pp. 1, 17, 20, 25 and figs 10, 11.

40. ibid., pp. 16-17.

41. Roesdahl, Else and Wilson, D. M., ed., *From Viking to Crusader: the Scandinavians and Europe 800-1200*, Nordic Council of Ministers, Uddevalla 1992, pp. 146, 275.

42. Sawyer, 'Process of Scandinavian christianization', p. 71.

43. Warren, W. L., *Henry II*, Eyre Methuen, London 1973, pp. 100, 163-4.

44. Bill, Jan, 'Ships and seamanship' in Sawyer, Peter, ed., *The Oxford Illustrated History of the Vikings*, Oxford University Press, Oxford and New York 1997, pp. 192-3.

45. Christensen, A.-E., 'Ship graffiti and models' in Wallace, P. F., ed., *Miscellanea I*, Royal Irish Academy, Dublin 1988, pp. 13-26.

46. Lang, J. T., *Viking-age Decorated Wood: a Study of its Ornament and Style*, Royal Irish Academy, Dublin 1988.

47. ibid., pp. 63-5 and figs 70-1; plate XIII.

48. Barnes, M. P., Hagland, J. R. and Page, R. I., *The Runic Inscriptions of Viking Age Dublin*, Royal Irish Academy, Dublin 1997.

49. ibid., pp. 14-15.

50. Ó Corráin, Donnchadh, 'Viking Ireland – afterthoughts' in Clarke, H. B., Ní Mhaonaigh, Máire and Ó Floinn, Raghnall, ed., *Ireland and Scandinavia in the Early Viking Age*, Four Courts Press, Dublin 1998, pp. 449-52.

51. Parsons, D. N., 'How long did the Scandinavian language survive in England? Again' in Graham-Campbell, James, Hall, Richard, Jesch, Judith and Parsons, D. N., ed., *Vikings and the Danelaw: Select Papers from*

the Proceedings of the Thirteenth Viking Congress, Nottingham and York, 21-30 August 1997, Oxbow Books, Oxford 2001, pp. 299-312.

52. Doherty, Charles, 'The Vikings in Ireland: a review' in Clarke, H. B., Ní Mhaonaigh, Máire and Ó Floinn, Raghnall, ed., *Ireland and Scandinavia in the Early Viking Age*, Four Courts Press, Dublin 1998, pp. 298-300.

53. McLoughlin, E. P., *Report on the Anatomical Investigation of the Skeletal Remains unearthed at Castleknock in the Excavation of an Early Christian Cemetery in the Summer of 1938*, Stationery Office, Dublin 1950, pp. iii, iv, 71.

54. Conway, Malachy, *Director's First Findings from Excavations in Cabinteely*, Margaret Gowen & Co., Glenageary 1999, pp. 20-34.

55. McLoughlin, *Report on the Anatomical Investigation*, p. v.

56. *AU*, pp. 276-7.

57. Wamers, Egon, 'Insular finds in Viking Age Scandinavia and the state formation of Norway' in Clarke, H. B., Ní Mhaonaigh, Máire and Ó Floinn, Raghnall, ed., *Ireland and Scandinavia in the Early Viking Age*, Four Courts Press, Dublin 1998, pp. 37-59 and fig. 2.3.

58. ibid., pp. 38, 42-3.

59. Bates, David, *Normandy before 1066*, Longman, London and New York 1982, p. 21.

60. Wood, 'Christians and pagans', p. 54; cf. Abrams, 'Conversion of the Scandinavians', pp. 19-21.

61. Smyth, A. P., *Scandinavian York and Dublin: the History and Archaeology of Two Related Viking Kingdoms*, 2 vols, Templekiernan Press and Humanities Press, Dublin and New Jersey 1975-9; reprinted as 2 vols in 1, Irish Academic Press, Dublin 1987, Vol 2, pp. 107-25, 156-72.

62. Angus, W. S., 'Christianity as a political force in Northumbria in the Danish and Norse periods' in Small, Alan, ed., *The Fourth Viking Congress*, Oliver and Boyd, Edinburgh and London 1965, pp. 155-8; cf. Whitelock, Dorothy, 'The conversion of the eastern Danelaw', *Saga-Book of the Viking Society* XII (1937-45), p. 161.

63. Sawyer, 'Process of Scandinavian christianization', p. 69.

64. Foote, Peter and Wilson, D. M., *The Viking Achievement: the Society and Culture of Early Medieval Scandinavia*, Sidgwick and Jackson, London 1970, p. 60.

65. Clarke, 'Conversion, church and cathedral', fig. 3.

66. Sawyer, 'Process of Scandinavian christianization', p. 68.

67. Mac Erlean, John, 'Synod of Ráith Breasail: Boundaries of the dioceses of Ireland (AD 1110 or 1118)', *Archivium Hibernicum* III (1914), pp. 3, 5, 11, 16.

68. Gwynn, Aubrey, 'The Synod of Kells, 1152' in *The Irish Church in the Eleventh and Twelfth Centuries*, ed. Gerard O'Brien, Four Courts Press, Blackrock 1992, pp. 228-30.

Delivered 5 February 2002

The Development of the Medieval Papacy

Michael Haren

I should like to preface my reflections on the subject by com-memorating the late Rev Prof F. X. Martin, OSA, who was a staunch friend of this place and of its environs and who would undoubtedly have been an enthusiastic supporter of the present lecture series – the more for that our proceedings are being con-ducted at precisely the subterranean level which so stirred his energies.[1]

I begin with some observations on method. Unlike Professor Freyne, I am both by training and professional engagement a historian and my focus is accordingly strictly on the past: not on what the past can teach the present (unless as regards the com-plexity of evidence generally and the utility accordingly of keep-ing the critical faculties acute) but simply and austerely on how the past may be correctly understood and authentically por-trayed. History that does not advert to the present is, indeed, doomed to be dead; the historian writes or speaks to the present and must find a means both of arresting present interest, even sympathy, and of rendering his dull matter intelligible in pre-sent terms. The more remote the period, the more difficult the undertaking, not least as regards the latter dimension. In a theo-logical or ecclesiological frame, the restriction of focus, however, means that the historian remains on the perimeter. Though he may well long to canter through the more verdant pastures of theory and relevance himself, his function is rather with the hedges, repairing a hole here, cropping over-luxuriant veget-ation there, at his most intrusive erecting a few strands of barbed wire. Where, as is sometimes the case, theological statements are contingent on a historical understanding, the historian comes into his own in setting the parameters, but he does not himself by profession make theological statements, certainly. Among the many hazards of his own discipline, he may count himself fortunate to succeed in making viable historical statements.

With that preliminary, I approach – in necessarily selective and glancing fashion – the medieval phase of the longest surviving institution of western Europe. There is no time for a detailed canvas. My aim is broad brushstrokes. I find myself, accordingly, making a few rather obvious remarks. One is that the papacy – whatever view, theologically or ecclesiologically, be taken of its origin or place in the grand providential scheme – is in its workaday functioning (which as regards the past means its history) a human institution, peopled by mere mortals, who bring to their mission, besides their personal strengths and weaknesses, the insights and conventions of their time. With that datum the historian feels utterly at home: he is apt to be shocked and expects to be edified precisely in the measure that human conduct and human reactions to contemporary pressures shock or edify. More, and he risks abandoning history for polemic or apologetic.

I begin properly by remarking, not I hope wholly simplistically, that the pope is bishop of Rome. A few years ago I was present at on all counts a highly memorabledinner party where the discussion moved to the so-called prophecies of Malachy – there is no knowing where Dublin dinner-party conversation will end up – and the potentially disconcerting observation that there are, I understand, only two more popes listed.[2] One of the other guests ingeniously suggested that this might mean no more than that thenceforth the papacy's functions would be discharged by committee. The prospect in context met with rather more enthusiasm than the charismatic properties of a committee régime might in general be held to warrant. To each his own definition of cataclysm! The fact that the loss to the diocese of Rome (whatever about the church universal) in this transition, and its implications by analogy, passed without comment is a fair indication of how far one rôle has eclipsed the other. In a sense, and for a television age, the modern pope belongs to the

world: fundamentally, however, he is what his earliest prede-
cessors were, bishop of a see – a see, of course, with a very particular history and claims.

It might seem superfluous in Christ Church Cathedral to emphasise that the pope is bishop of Rome, since the term was
much used in Reformation argument to curtail the universalist
pretensions which were so large a part of the developed medieval papacy. It both is, however, central to understanding the
papal office and for the historian constitutes a significant part of
the reality. In understanding the office, for – not least – it is by
virtue of that fact that the papacy is to this day an elective office.
As most of you will know, the leaders of the early Christian as-
semblies were chosen by the community of believers – originally,
it would appear, in such a way as to leave maximum room for
the operation of the Spirit: later the Spirit came to be channelled
a little. In the early middle ages election, often of a rough-and-
ready or determinedly enthusiastic kind, was the route by
which bishops were appointed. We have relatively well-known
late-antique examples of enthusiastic episcopal election in the
cases of Ambrose of Milan and Augustine of Hippo. In the case
of the pope, we may recall that arch-reformer, Gregory VII
(Hildebrand), who, in the tumultuous proceeding during the
funeral of his predecessor on 22 April 1073, was seized and
'dragged to the place of apostolic rule', a compliment that
proved inconvenient, since he championed orderly election. In
time, the elective procedure in the case of bishops generally devolved on a body of senior clergy – the cathedral chapter in the
case of secular cathedrals, the monastic or quasi-monastic community in the case of regular. It was not until the fourteenth
century, in many respects the acme of medieval papal power,
that provision by the pope became the standard formal mecha-
nism by which an episcopal appointment was made, so routinely
that eventually it seemed that there was no other sound,
'catholic', way of becoming a bishop. I say 'formal', since in this
respect appearances may deceive: no more than theoretically
'free election' was papal provision of bishops in practice, typi-

cally, unfettered. The procedure was especially well defined in a habitually strong monarchy like medieval England's: on occurrence of a vacancy, the chapter sought the *congé d'élire* (the king's permission to elect); from that point the royal officers maintained a close vigilance over the proceedings; the result was usually, in a see worth the trouble, a candidate of the king's choice, duly elected by the chapter and signified to the pope; the pope then, in what was, on the face of it only, a spontaneous procedure, issued a bull addressed to the candidate, recapitulating how the fact of vacancy had come to his notice, how he had had close and long consultation with the cardinals whom to appoint and how his choice had fallen on the surprised addressee. Whatever the arguments for or against the method of episcopal appointment in the modern Church of England, a version of it is of respectable antiquity. 'Respectable' is no redundant adjective for many of these 'Caesarean prelates' were thoroughly worthy men, whose reputation grows with the advance of historical research into their contribution.

By contrast and somewhat paradoxically, the papacy itself – though by no means immune to contextual pressure – remained (there being no superior ecclesiastical interest active) both formally and, overall, more or less effectively elective. Even here, though, it would be simplistic to imply an undeviating line of development. Pope Symmachus, for example, in the early sixth century, treats the pope as being negligent if he fails to designate his successor. Election, however, triumphed: from the middle of the thirteenth century by the distinctive method of the conclave (essentially locking the cardinals up and not letting them out until they did the business, a typically concrete medieval stratagem designed to overcome their reluctance on occasion to reach the decision which, once made, for the time reduced their influence and saddled them with a master). The cardinals, reductively, *qua* electors, are in highly formalised fashion acting as the representatives of the Christian community of the diocese of Rome, of which by virtue of their titular churches they are senior members.

To remain for the moment with this local dimension: a great deal of what the historian is confronted with as the importance of the papacy in the early centuries is humdrum. (If man does not live by bread alone, he certainly does not live without it.) In choosing vignettes of papal activity on this level, one would perhaps present the pope and his clergy boating across a flooded Campo Marzio (the area round the Pantheon) to bring emergency supplies to his diocesans or Pope St Gregory the Great housing the refugees from the Lombard devastation of northern Lazio.[3] In this respect, the early papacy resembles, *mutatis mutandis*, the papacy of the seventeenth, eighteenth and early nineteenth centuries in its rôle as the government of the papal states. This rôle had a severely bad press in the nineteenth century, especially within liberal England – in its deeply seated antipathy to absolutism as much as in its commitment to Reformed religion – and within post-Risorgimento Italy, where liberalism was compounded by a nationalistic fervour the more strident for that most new 'Italians' remained provincial at heart and suspicious at best of the Savoyard order. Long out of fashion, *ancien régime* papal government is still historiographically a relatively neglected subject. However, its effects cannot be missed by the tourist in Rome who is not deterred by Latin inscriptions: Pope x decreed the provision of a fountain here; Pope y improved access to the city there; Pope z beautified this piazza by erecting the central obelisk. Not long ago, when the matter was acutely topical, William Rees-Mogg in *The Times* signalled how the régime of contiguous slaughter still, if somewhat controversially, practised for the control of foot and mouth disease, originated in the method adopted in the early nineteenth-century papal states. Within the constraints of a short lecture, it would be disproportionate to spend long on the routine practicality of papal government. I have for convenience recalled it mainly by reference to the more palpable, modern monuments to it, but a review which ignored it would miss a literally vital element of the historical composition of the papacy both in the middle ages and long beyond.

I should observe that – paradoxically in view of its later perceived importance – the wider governmental side was forced on
the papacy, by the collapse of imperial administration. There
was no point at which the Roman empire formally ended. When
the western half ceased to have its own emperor, authority devolved theoretically on the Emperor proper, ensconced in the
Greek city of Constantinople or Byzantium. Justinian recovered
Italy from the Ostrogoths in the mid-sixth century but, apart
from a central corridor between Rome and the naval base of
Ravenna, Byzantine rule had by the seventh century ceased to
function in the face of the Lombard invasion. The only institution that remained with a plausible capacity to fill the gap was
the papacy and it filled it with loud complaint against the failure
of the emperor in the East to do his job (rather as the inhabitants
of the diminished lordship of Ireland in the fifteenth century
complained at the way in which the king was frequently perceived as abandoning them to their own devices in the face of
the surrounding threat from the Gaelic resurgence). The papacy
saw an alternative to being a neglected appendage: in the course
of the eighth century it accomplished a revolution, progressively
detaching itself from the East and on Christmas Day 800 crown-
ing a new emperor in the West – Charlemagne. In the revived
western empire it hoped to have a protector. In fact, as has often
been observed, it had created a monster. The western emperor
threatened at crucial periods to reduce the papacy to a purely
localised rôle, though it must also be said that in the early
eleventh century he was responsible for liberating it from the
stranglehold of the Roman nobility and setting it on the path of a
reform programme whose effects continue to shape clerical life.

Nearly related to the local governmental dimension, but on
the ecclesiastical rather than the secular side, is the early papacy's
rôle in church-building. As Professor Freyne pointed out last
week, Constantine commenced the process. Indeed, he had had
to find a new architectural language for the enterprise, since before his time Christianity had made no architectural impact on
the city – ecclesiastical activities being conducted in what were

both legally and structurally private houses. For his purpose, he
adopted the basilica – formerly a secular, commercial genre. An
important point about Constantinian church-building is that,
unlike the emperor's most successful venture, St Peter's, where
the site was dictated by the tradition of the apostle's burial place,
the foundation of St John at the Lateran – technically the more
important, being the cathedral church of Rome – was something
of a white elephant. Before he was a Christian (in the formal
sense at least – he was not baptised until his deathbed),
Constantine was an emperor. A markedly adroit emperor, who
ruled for over thirty years, he knew a thing or two about politics.
One of the things he knew was the advantage, if at all possible,
of not losing old adherents as you acquired new and he managed this by the time-honoured device of sending different,
even contradictory, signals to different constituencies of supporter. The magnificent church of St John at the Lateran was
conceptually complex. Not only was it on imperial land, and
thus easier on the imperial purse; it was triumphantly raised on
the former headquarters of his rival Maxentius' guard. That was
one factor in its siting. It was also as removed as it could be from
the centre of the city. To the extent that it thereby sought to
avoid offending the still vigorous pagan lobby, it rendered itself
also a largely impractical venue for the bishop's ministering to
his flock. Hence the need for the popes themselves to build
churches which would serve as what came to be called the stations
of the city. We have several cases in the fourth century to suggest that, as with secular public officials, popes may even have
been chosen, from time to time at least, with some consideration
for their having personal resources adequate to the discharge of
the heavy financial burdens involved. The examples are to the
point of Pope Mark (336), whose foundation of the first church
of S. Marco (near the present-day Piazza Venezia) was on family
property, and of Pope Damasus I (366-384), the scion of an ecclesiastical family, whose estate on the site of the present
Renaissance Palazzo della Cancelleria is preserved in the name
of the adjacent church of San Lorenzo in Damaso. The rôle is

well displayed in the appearance of Pope Felix IV, off-centre-
stage in the great sixth-century mosaic in which Sts Peter and
Paul present the martyred Sts Cosmas and Damian to the majes-
tic Christ of the Parousia in the church dedicated to them,
thought to be the converted audience hall of the classical city
prefect, on the edge of the Roman forum.[4]

The universalist dimension of the papacy is intimately linked
to the local. It grew particularly from the see of Rome's determi-
nation not to be diminished by the shift (in 324) of the empire's
political capital to Constantinople and by its exploitation of its
apostolic status to that end. On the level of nomenclature, the
terms 'Roman church' and 'apostolic see' – not 'papacy' nor, still
less, 'Vatican' – are the medieval language of reference. They
continued to be employed even when the papacy was for long
periods resident elsewhere, as in its sojourn at Avignon for approximately the first seven decades of the fourteenth century.
As has been said of the hedgehog, the early medieval popes had
one big idea and it is no small part of their success that they canvassed it in season and out of season – that they were the heirs of
St Peter and enjoyed the primacy for which the exegesis of Mt
16:18-19 (Peter and the keys) and Jn 21:16-17 ('Feed my sheep')
served as the crucial foundation, conferring on Rome an advantage over those several other sees with a claim to apostolic origins. 'Tu es Petrus' ('You are Peter') proclaims the cupola of New
St Peter's, in Paul V's inspired positioning of the 'Confessio Petri'
(as Peter's declaration of faith came to be known). It is the grand
culmination of the text's application over many centuries. Even
the papal style, 'servant of the servants of God', known from the
time of Gregory the Great though not consistently established as
a diplomatic feature until the ninth century, notwithstanding its
overt humility, conveys a subtext from Mt 20:27: 'He who would
be first among you shall be the servant of all.' The impact of the
concept of 'heir of Peter' can be measured best perhaps by its
penetration to the periphery, in the Irish term 'coarb of Peter'
applied to the pope, and the prestige of 'apostolic see', as stemming from its traditional custody of the tombs of the apostles

Peter and Paul, in the secondary meaning 'burial place' attaching to the Irish term '*róm*'.

In Roman law, the heir replaced the deceased. What being 'heir of Peter' meant in practice was a matter of elaboration. St Columbanus, addressing Pope Boniface IV in 613, put it to him bluntly that Peter got his authority by the rectitude of his confession.[5] Some historians have read an insinuation that authority could be lost by heterodoxy.[6] However, even on the very issue of the Celtic church's self-confident stand as regards the Easter question, the trend was clear: at the Synod of Whitby in 664, King Oswiu was represented as asking whether Columba had received authority similar to that of the Apostle Peter, and, deferring to Mt 16:18-19, professed his unwillingness to quarrel with the warden of heaven's gate.[7] Key-bearer (with implication of power to include and exclude) and supreme pastor became the most frequent metaphors of the papal office. 'Bridge-builder' (the literal meaning thought to underly the title '*pontifex maximus*' or 'supreme pontiff', inherited from pagan religion) was strangely neglected, despite its possibilities to our minds.

The elaboration to which I refer was cumulative. Already by the early sixth century, a synod held by Pope Symmachus I (to whom I have referred for his views on the papal succession) accepted his contention that the apostolic see could be judged by no one. The circumstances were colourful: Symmachus was in deep trouble both from a rival claim and over his relationship with a lady the various possible renderings of whose name, Conditaria – 'Spicy',[8] 'Saucy' or 'Hot Stuff' – convey well enough the nature of his congregation's misgivings. But as Yeats insists that great poetry takes its rise from the unlikeliest prompting, so does crisis force the application of far-reaching theory. The medieval papacy's strength was in garnering the past (somewhat creatively in Symmachus' case) and in the development of law. This latter had two sources. On the one hand, it was demand-led. From the high middle ages on, a flood of knotty problems from all over western Christendom came to the popes for resolution and the resultant replies were collected for future reference as 'decretal letters'. The second source was scholarly, the product of the medieval universities – of which the popes were one of the most significant patrons, both as sources of privilege and, through the grant of licences for study, in providing a system of what were effectively bursaries. Many late medieval popes had themselves been teaching or practising lawyers. A notable example is Sinibaldo dei Fieschi, formerly a master at the great law university of Bologna and a judge-auditor at the curia, who as Pope Innocent IV (1243-1254) made time to continue his work of commentary on the legal sources, including even – with the engaging flash of enthusiastic approval – his own enactments. This was no narcissism. It epitomises rather the rational, jurisprudential, as opposed to arbitrarily prescriptive, dynamic of the greater part of the medieval canonical tradition. If the highest office was itself remarkably open to raw ability that was *a fortiori* true of the administrative apparatus by which it was supported. As the late Professor Ullmann justly observed, 'No other European government in the thirteenth or fourteenth centuries had such a cosmopolitan galaxy of talent, learning and practical experience as the papacy.'[9] The strength was however also capable of being a weakness. The law thus emanating regulated all aspects of church affairs except the apex. Rather, indeed, it emphasised that the apex was incapable of regulation: 'If the temporal power errs', says Boniface VIII in his bull *Unam Sanctam* (1302), 'it shall be judged by the spiritual power. If the lesser spiritual power errs its judge is its superior. But if the highest spiritual power errs, it can be judged by God alone and not by man, as the apostle testifies (1 Cor 2:15), "He that is spiritual judges all things, yet he himself is judged of no man".'[10] Symmachus' principle had by now been massively underpinned by the quasi-apostolic doctrine and Neoplatonist cosmic analysis of pseudo-Dionysius, in whose universe dominion below was a reflection of and indissolubly linked to dominion above. The elaborated hierocratic theory constituted an assertion of the church's independence and sovereignty set against the encroachment of a medieval version of secularism – though

the term in medieval reference lacks its modern import.[11]
Secular rulers were no less jealous of their sovereignty and independence and dissented forcefully and effectively from the
worldview adopted by Boniface as it concerned them. My outline of the working of episcopal provision may be cited as a re-
minder that medieval theory and practice might widely diverge
– or, to put the matter otherwise, that rival theories and models
more often than not converged in an undramatic compromise
which suited the principal parties tolerably well. The implications for internal, ecclesiastical, government of what Boniface
was articulating proved more acute. The constitutional issue
within the church became critical in the Great Schism (1378-
1415) when two and eventually three rival lines of popes split
western Christendom. In the legal vacuum, a new theory had to
be painfully worked out for the resolution of the problem. That
theory was conciliarism which, at the Council of Constance, declared in the decree 'Sacrosancta' the primacy of a council over
the pope. Conciliarism however, despite its success in resolving
the schism and the interest and importance of the doctrine that it
had developed, found itself outmanoeuvred by the papacy
which it had restored and it eventually fell apart in dissension.

   That the late medieval papacy developed into a mighty administrative edifice, the first pan-European government since
Roman imperial times, was a cause of dismay, even scandal, to
many reforming minds of the middle ages themselves. The history of the Franciscan Order would, did time allow, be of special
interest in this regard. Yet, the papacy's patronage at an early
stage was a vital element in the success of the mendicant ideal
with which the Franciscans identified the truly apostolic life.
The consideration cautions against posing these antitheses too
starkly. The history of the medieval church is awash with such
cross-currents, which threaten to run in and swamp too ready
moralising. Before Boniface VIII – a paradigm of the lawyer-
pope, though his many opponents, not least those within the
college of cardinals itself, were less restrained in their character-
isation – comes the *ingenu* hermit-pope, Celestine V. Celestine's

miserable end and the deterrent example that he came to represent, as the only pope to make what Dante, in ferocious disparagement, called the 'great refusal' of abdication, should not be allowed to overshadow the desperate boldness of the experiment that his election constituted. By the same token, it is necessary to emphasise that in very large measure the construction of the administrative edifice too was demand-led rather than being the product of conscious policy. Take for example the thousands of papal letters that survive in the Vatican Archives for late medieval Ireland. These are not the imposition of 'Rome-rule' on the Irish church but the results of the unremitting application to the papal curia on the part of Irish clerics, pursuing for the most part their disputed title to benefices locally. (As such they are for the historian an irreplaceable source of richly detailed information for a period and for areas that are otherwise largely undocumented. Their value is related precisely to the fact that the business contained in them stems from circumstances on the ground – not from a distant view of how matters were or should be.)

These Irish clerics or their proctors joined throngs of their counterparts from all over Europe in the papal antechambers. There was never an opportune time, from a high-governmental or crudely economic viewpoint, to bring this system to an end. The Council of Constance tried and failed. The case is instructive of that Renaissance pope who has long stood in the popular mind as the most infamous symbol of the decline of the institution, Alexander VI (Borgia). The naked self-indulgence of his dynastic ambitions is the major sin that survives unequivocally from critical scrutiny of his pontificate. As regards his having progeny whose interests to promote, the mainstream of contemporary Irish secular clerical opinion would hardly have viewed that as scandalous: the familial character of the Irish church has left disproportionately heavy impress on the Roman sources.[12] Much of the more exotic colouring of his court proves disappointingly evanescent or pales into uncertainty under the light of investigation. Within the themes that jostle for attention, the historian (if thoroughly reconciled to the prospect that his titles

should languish on the bookshelves) would find it in some degree enlightening to examine the striking series of administrative reforms by which Alexander set his hand to render trans-
parent the processes of his government and to cut into the venal
official structure maintained by the flow of dispensations and
graces from his chancery.

> Placed by divine disposition in the watchtower of the apos-
> tolic see, we are exercised in the whole engagement of the
> mind over the reform of morals, so that, in accordance with
> the ministry of the pastoral office, we might pluck out what
> needs to be plucked out and plant what should be planted.
> For we have noted that current morals have insidiously parted
> stream from the ancient discipline and, breaking through
> those old and salutary establishments of the sacred councils
> and the supreme pontiffs by which lust and avarice were re-
> strained, have burst forth into a licence that must be tolerated
> no longer. Prone indeed is the nature of mortal men to evil
> and appetite does not at all times submit to reason, but, as the
> apostle has it, it leads the mind captive and the people into
> the law of sin.[13]

'Quite so', one might echo. However, if 'the whole engagement of the mind' seems a trifle exaggerated of Alexander's pre-
occupation with morals, what follows in some five thousand
words of detailed provisions may not be regarded as merely
cynical. Even the fluent – dare one say 'watery'? – proem is far
from being otherwise unexampled in its reflection of a capacity
for operating on levels where pragmatism and idealism are detached, or are associated only at a level of the pyschology that, as
regards the past, is rarely within scope of objective inquiry. In
considering Alexander's departure, the historian is brought to
dwell on the implications of the fact that the bold attempt petered
out, in the face equally of vested interest and of the determin-
ation of petitioners, almost immediately it had been promulgated
– faltering as might an assault in our own time on the West's
consumption of energy or its output of carbon dioxide. Failed
and even half-hearted initiatives can, though, be revelatory.

Underneath the dominant resonance of Alexander VI's sex-life (actually rather staid, it would seem) or the political ruthlessness of his son, Cesare Borgia (immortalised by Machiavelli), is this more muffled, ultimately stifled, beat. The historical import is distinctly ambivalent. While it is noteworthy that Alexander was – at least intermittently – conscious that things could not continue as they were, it is no less so that he was (his personal attachments aside) effectively trapped within the plenitude of power that he theoretically wielded. The combination of higher reflection – even in what might seem this least likely instance – and remorselessly mechanistic bureaucratic functioning captures something that is authentic of the late medieval papacy as an institution.

Notes

1. The audience had for the occasion adjourned to the crypt.

2. A calculation now altered by the death in the interval of Pope John Paul II

3. I am indebted here and in other reflections both on the rôle of the popes in the life of the medieval city and the particulars of its fabric to the masterly account of Krautheimer, *Rome*.

4. See Krautheimer, *Rome*, pp. 33, 71.

5. Columbanus, Letter 5; ed. and tr. Walker, *Sancti Columbani Opera*, pp. 48-51, for the relevant passages.

6. The matter has been judiciously reviewed by Bracken, 'Authority and duty', who draws attention to the emphasis on right judgement.

7. The debate is recounted in Bede, *Ecclesiastical History*, 3. 25.

8. The suggestion of Professor Henry Chadwick.

9. Ullmann, *Law and Politics*, p. 146.

10. Friedberg, *Corpus Iuris Canonici*, vol. 2, 1245-6. The translation quoted is that of Tierney, *The Crisis of Church and State*, p. 189.

11. The best statement of the trend is the classic study, Lagarde, *La Naissance de l'Esprit Laique*.

12. See Haren, 'Social Structures of the Irish Church'.

13. The complete Latin text of these remarkable ordinances is edited in Tangl, *Die päpstlichen Kanzleiordnungen*.

Bibliography

Bracken, D., 'Authority and duty: Columbanus and the primacy of Rome', *Peritia. Journal of the Medieval Academy of Ireland* XVI (2002), pp. 168-213

Friedberg, E., *Corpus Iuris Canonici*, vol. 2 , Bernard Tauchnitz, Leipzig, 1881

Haren, M. J., 'Social structures of the Irish Church. A new source in papal penitentiary dispensations for illegitimacy', in L. Schmugge, ed., *Illegitimät im Spätmittelalter*, Schriften des historischen Kollegs, Kolloquien XXIX, R. Oldenbourg Verlag, Munich 1994, pp. 207-226

Krautheimer, R., *Rome: Portrait of a City*, 312-1308, Princeton University Press, Princeton, N. J. 1980

Lagarde, G., *La Naissance de l'Esprit Laique au Déclin du Moyen Age*, 3rd edition, Editions Béatrice, Louvain 1956-1970

Tangl, M., *Die päpstlichen Kanzleiordnungen von 1200-1500*, Innsbruck 1894, reprinted Scientia, Aalen 1959

Tierney, B., *The Crisis of Church and State 1050-1300*, Prentice-Hall Inc., Englewood Cliffs, N. J., 1964

Ullmann, W., *Law and Politics in the Middle Ages*, The Sources of History Ltd, London 1975

Walker, G. S. M., *Sancti Columbani Opera*, Scriptores Latini Hibernici II, Dublin Institute for Advanced Studies, Dublin 1970

Delivered 16 October 2001

The Reformation of the Irish church in the Twelfth Century

Marie Therese Flanagan

The Irish church underwent a major transformation in the twelfth century which is described conventionally as 'the twelfth-century reform movement' though arguably the changes wrought were much more fundamental than that title suggests. It was not merely a case of reforming existing practices or structures, but rather a radical substitution of entirely new institutions and observances. In the context of 2000 years of Christianity, one way of interpreting the changes brought about in the Irish church in the course of the twelfth century is to view the process as one of Europeanisation, or rather re-Europeanisation: a regional church that had developed its own customs was brought into greater conformity with contemporary European norms.

The Christian church in Ireland from its origins in the fifth century was, of course, part of western Latin Christendom. Ireland was the first country in western Europe to be converted to Christianity without the formal agency of the Roman empire. Ireland had not been Romanised by the legions of Rome, but by being Christianised, it was brought into much closer association with the Roman and post-Roman culture of the European mainland. Christianity brought not just a new religion but also a new culture, writing and literacy, and the Latin language, all of which were to have a dramatic impact on Irish culture. By that very fact alone, the introduction of Christianity led to a process of Europeanisation, from the fifth century onwards, of Irish society and of its distinctively Celtic culture. The twelfth century was another formative period in which externally driven change impacted on Irish society. The changes brought about in the Irish church in the course of the twelfth century transformed the

institutional structures, the liturgy, and more broadly Irish religious culture. The Latin language, the universal language of
western Christendom, was re-instated in the twelfth century as
the language of liturgy and public worship at the expense of the
vernacular which had played an important role in the early Irish
church. There was also a transformation of architecture with the
introduction of new types of church buildings and monasteries,
and new styles, firstly the Romanesque and later the Gothic
style. Christ Church Cathedral, Dublin, is one important graphic
testimony to the architectural innovations of the twelfth century.
The twelfth-century changes resulted in a local church that had
developed regional customs and particularist practices, which
distinguished it from the European heartland, being brought
into closer harmony with western Latin Christendom.

Western, or Latin, Christendom may be defined as the multi-
tude of churches worshipping in Latin according to a more or
less similar liturgical rite. In practice, there had been marked regional diversity in the early medieval period, even though uniformity and harmony of the *Christianus populus* had been the
ideal. Beginning in the eleventh century, however, a greater in-
sistence on uniformity developed, and the bishop of Rome, or
the institution of the papacy as it came to be called, took on a
more directive role which became more determined and effective as the eleventh century progressed. Since the very birth of
official western Christianity, inaugurated by the conversion of
the Roman Emperor Constantine in AD 315, and consolidated in
395 when the Emperor Theodosius outlawed pagan religions
and declared Christianity to be the official religion of the Roman
Empire, the bishop of Rome, as the head of the only church in
the West which had been founded by an apostle, Peter, had enjoyed a position of honorific prestige in western Europe. In the
course of the eleventh century that long-standing prestige was
transformed into a governmental role. A papal administration
was elaborated, papal decisions became more enforceable and,
as a result, institutional and liturgical uniformity more prevailing. The processes of change were not uniform throughout

Europe, and one can usefully distinguish between a core or met-ropolitan region, in which change proceeded rapidly, and a per-iphery that took longer to adapt. Ireland lay on the periphery, and the transformations of church and society that are such a noticeable feature of the European mainland from about 1050 onwards reached Ireland later, and proceeded more slowly, and did not begin to make a substantive difference until the second half of the twelfth century.

The expanding geographical range of the papacy, and its ac-tive intervention in local churches, is signalled by a letter ad-dressed by Pope Gregory VII about 1085 to Toirrdelbach Ua Briain, king of Munster, and aspiring high-king. It is the first ex-tant papal letter to Ireland since a letter of 640 that had been sent to the Irish church by Pope-elect John IV in the context of the seventh-century controversy over the calculation of the date of Easter. Pope Gregory's letter emphasised the role of the bishop of Rome as the successor of Peter, to whom as Gregory wrote to Toirrdelbach Ua Briain, 'the whole world owed obedience and reverence'; and Gregory urged the Irish king 'to be mindful ever devoutly to revere and obey the Holy Roman church' and to consult him if any matters of doubt had arisen which required clarification.[1] The letter well demonstrates the expanding range of the papacy as it redefined its role and widened its geographi-cal horizons. The number of papal letters sent to Ireland in-creased steadily from the twelfth century onwards.

The impact of the new interventionist papacy on the Irish church can also be traced in the developing role of papal legates and papally convened church councils, both on the continent and in Ireland. The first church council convened in Ireland at the behest of a papal legate was the Synod of Kells in 1152, presided over by Cardinal John Paparo. Even before special papal emissaries travelled from Rome to Ireland, individual Irish churchmen had come into contact with the reformist papacy by travelling to the continent, and had been appointed as native papal legates, that is as the pope's resident representative in Ireland. Gillebertus, bishop of Limerick, is attested already in the first decade of the twelfth century as native papal legate. Gillebertus' appointment must have resulted from a visit that he had made to the continent, the circumstances of which remain unknown, but from correspondence between him and Anselm, archbishop of Canterbury, we learn that the two men had met in Normandy.[2]

Gillebertus was to be succeeded by the better-known St Malachy, the most prominent Irish churchman of the first half of the twelfth century. Traditionally known as Malachy of Armagh he was in turn bishop of Connor, then for a very brief period archbishop of Armagh, from which office he resigned in 1136 to become bishop of Down. Malachy was appointed native papal legate on the occasion of his first visit to Rome in 1139 to attend a Lateran council that had been convened by Pope Innocent II. It was while on his way to another papally convened church council in 1148 that Malachy took ill and died and was buried in the Cistercian monastery of Clairvaux in Burgundy. Malachy was to become the first papally canonised, or externally validated, saint of the Irish church. His canonisation in 1190 may be regarded as an illustration of the Europeanisation of the Irish church.[3]

The two journeys that Malachy undertook to the continent in 1139 and 1148 are symptomatic of a more active Irish engagement with the continental church. The Irish had been intrepid travellers to the continent in the early medieval period as missionaries and scholars, but the intrusion of the Vikings into the British Isles in the late eighth century had disrupted established travel patterns. It was not until the eleventh century that relative peace returned to the European seaboards and sea travel could be resumed safely. A series of Irish pilgrimages to Rome to the shrine of St Peter made by Irish churchmen and kings is recorded in the eleventh century in the annals, the year by year records that were kept in the more important Irish churches. In the pre-Viking period Irish activity on the continent is known primarily from continental sources. We learn nothing from Irish sources, for example, about the great Irish missionary, Columbanus, who established a number of important monasteries in France,

Switzerland, and Italy. From the eleventh century onwards, as Irish travel to the continent resumed and increased, not only was foreign news brought back by travellers to Ireland, but Irish scribes found it sufficiently relevant to incorporate it into their annals. Annalistic entries recording external events are symptomatic of an increase in the frequency of traffic between Ireland and the continent, as well as a more active Irish interest and engagement in continental affairs. It was as a result of a pilgrimage to Rome undertaken in 1028[4] by the Hiberno-Norse king, Sitriuc, that the mixed Hiberno-Scandinavian population of Dublin received its first bishop, Dúnán, and the early stages in the building of Christ Church Cathedral were begun. Continental journeys would have brought home to individual Irish churchmen and kings the organisational or structural differences between the continental church and their own by the twelfth century. The impetus for change was not solely driven by the external agency of the papacy. Equally important was the recognition by Irish clergy, and even Irish kings, of the differences of their church and their willingness and desire to conform. As a result of these impulses for change, the product both of external exhortation and Irish initiative, the existing institutions of the Irish church were re-structured in the course of the twelfth century.

One of the most important areas of structural change related to bishops and dioceses. Christianity in the West had developed its organisational structures within the political and social context of the late fourth-century Roman empire, in which bishoprics had been city-based and heavily dependent on urban institutions. In the overwhelmingly rural society of fifth-century Ireland, by contrast, bishops had not necessarily had a fixed seat or cathedral church; they had tended to shift with changing political circumstances, and to take their titles from a political grouping or a region rather than the location of their see or cathedral church. It would be wrong to think, however, that bishops had not been important in the pre-twelfth-century Irish church. In the past it has been suggested that episcopal authority was supplanted in the early Irish church by monastic institutions. That was never the case: the bishop remained the highest ecclesiastical authority and his unique episcopal functions of or-dination of clergy, consecration of fellow bishops, and conferral of the sacrament of confirmation were never usurped by monas-tic abbots.[5] What primarily distinguished the Irish episcopate from its continental counterparts was the lack of fixed sees and stable diocesan boundaries and that was to be remedied in the twelfth century.

Bishops and dioceses were the natural starting point for structural change since church leadership, the training and supervision of clergy, and the provision of pastoral services to the laity, was the canonical duty of bishops. In 1111 a church council met at Ráith Bressail (Co Tipperary) under the auspices of Muirchertach Ua Briain, king of Munster and high-king, and drew up a scheme for an island-wide network of territorially de-limited dioceses with fixed sites designated in each diocese for the bishop's seat, or cathedral church. Twenty-four dioceses were proposed, encompassed within two archiepiscopal provinces of Armagh and of Cashel. It was important to gain papal confir-mation of the new diocesan structure, since one of the reasons for its establishment was to bring Irish church structures into greater conformity with the continental church. Papal approval was secured in 1152 at a synod held at Kells (Co Meath) presided over by the papal legate, Cardinal John Paparo. A major change between the Ráith Bressail scheme of 1111 and that of the Synod of Kells in 1152 was the creation of two addi-tional archiepiscopal provinces. The two-fold division between Armagh and Cashel, as proposed at Ráith Bressail, was amended by the additional creation of an archdiocese of Dublin and an archdiocese of Tuam, additions which reflected changes in the secular political landscape that had occurred in the intervening period. Also at the Synod of Kells, a clearly defined hierarchy of bishop, archbishop and primate was confirmed, with the arch-bishop of Armagh formally acknowledged as primate of the Irish church with a delegated authority from the pope. Irish archbishops henceforth were to travel to Rome to receive in person the *pallium* or pall, which was the symbol of their direct link with the papacy.

By 1152 the Irish church was structurally closer to that of its continental counterparts in that there was now in place an island-wide network of episcopal dioceses with fixed sees and fixed boundaries. The scheme that was papally approved at Kells in 1152, apart from minor local adjustments and modifications, remained stable for the rest of the medieval period. The arrangements endorsed by the papal legate at Kells broadly still form the basis of the diocesan boundaries of the Church of Ireland and to a lesser extent of the reconstituted dioceses of the post-Reformation Catholic church. The cathedral churches of the Church of Ireland are for the most part still located at sites approved at the Synod of Kells. The impact of that new diocesan structure is still visible in the many important twelfth-century churches that were built or restored and redecorated at the locations chosen to be episcopal sees. Major building programmes were inaugurated: Cormac's chapel on the Rock of Cashel provides an outstanding example of a prestigious building programme that was intended to reflect the new-found archiepiscopal status of Cashel. The establishment of a stable diocesan network was a significant achievement which can only be fully appreciated by a detailed analysis of the individual diocesan boundaries, and the way in which churchmen managed to accommodate the new episcopal structures to the political realities of twelfth-century Ireland. A large measure of compromise must have accompanied the scheme. There were winners and losers and some churches that made a bid for episcopal status failed to gain recognition as cathedral churches despite embarking on major building programmes (the churches of Roscrea in Co Tipperary and Ardmore in Co Waterford are two notable examples). The revolutionary impact of that restructuring should not be underestimated. The new cathedral churches had to be endowed with lands and income, and the greater part of the landed endowment would have come from redistributing the lands of other long-established churches, and particularly by reclaiming, or recovering lands that had fallen under lay control. It goes without saying that the bishops elected to serve in the newly constituted dioceses were to be canonically consecrated according to the same rite as their continental counterparts, and that their election was to be free from secular pressures, or interference from local families – abuses or deviations from canon law that had developed in the Irish church in the post-Viking period.

The next phase of the restructuring programme involved the further division of dioceses into a network of parochial churches to which were attached fixed parish boundaries, the parishioners of which were to pay first fruits, offerings and tithes to the designated parish church. Arguably, this marked a more innovative development than the restructuring of the episcopate, certainly from the standpoint of the laity. The novelty of the new parochial arrangements in relation to the Irish church is reflected in a treatise written by Bishop Gillebertus of Limerick, the native papal legate in Ireland, which was titled 'On the structure of the church'. Gillebertus described the church as a pyramid at the apex of which stood Christ and immediately below him the pope as Christ's representative on earth. At the base of the pyramid alongside the laity were monks who Gillebertus declared were called only to a life of prayer and ought not to minister to the laity since that was the responsibility of the priest of the parish, and like the secular clergy the monks were to be subject to episcopal authority.[6] The new parochial structures detailed by Gillebertus greatly enhanced the importance of the secular clergy and gave them for the first time something approaching parity of esteem with monks who had been regarded as the elite clergy in the early medieval period.

Irish monasticism was also to undergo change so as to bring it into greater conformity with Latin Christendom. The principal agency of change was the introduction of continental monastic observances in the form of the Cistercian and Augustinian rules. The first Cistercian monastery was established at Mellifont (Co Louth) in 1142. The Cistercian rule was based on the monastic rule of St Benedict that had been written in the mid-sixth century and which, by the tenth century, had become the normative rule for western monasticism not only on the continent but also in England. It had not, however, been adopted by the Irish church. That the rule of Benedict did not impact on the Irish church until the twelfth century is a good illustration of the way in which the Irish church had not followed developments on the European mainland. The Cistercians take their name from the mother-house founded in 1098 at Cîteaux, or Cistercium in its Latin form, in Burgundy. In the view of the Cistercians, the ideals of Benedict had become submerged under customs which were relaxed modifications that had resulted in a less spiritual, less ascetic lifestyle. The Cistercians sought a return to monastic austerity and simplicity in food, clothing, furnishings, and architecture. The distinctive features of Cistercian monasticism lay not only in the spiritual or internal life of the monastery, but also in structures of government that were developed to regulate uniformity of observance between Cistercian houses. Each Cistercian house was subject to another in a chain of dependence that led back ultimately to the mother-house of Cîteaux. Each community was to undergo an annual visitation or inspection, either from the abbot of the mother-house, or a delegated abbot of another Cistercian monastery. An annual chapter was held at Cîteaux that all Cistercian abbots were obliged to attend and which passed legislation that was binding on all Cistercian houses. The Cistercians fashioned administrative institutions that aimed at maintaining a uniform monastic observance. The Cistercians were the first truly international monastic order and were to be an important means of introducing to Ireland a greater conformity with monastic practices on the continent. By 1170 there were thirteen Cistercian houses in Ireland.

Another variety of continental monasticism introduced into the twelfth-century Irish church was the rule of St Augustine, a rule that was introduced into Christ Church Cathedral by Laurence O'Toole when he became archbishop of Dublin in 1162. Both observances – Cistercian and Augustinian – were promoted by Malachy of Armagh as a direct result of his first journey to the continent in 1139, where he had visited Cistercian and Augustinian communities. Augustinian houses were by far the most common in twelfth-century Ireland, exceeding in number the more high-profile Cistercian houses. By 1170 there were approximately forty houses observing the Augustinian rule in Ireland.

It is significant that Malachy was responsible for introducing both the Cistercian and Augustinian observances. He clearly saw them as having complementary roles to play in transforming Irish monastic observances. Malachy is recorded to have considered the Augustinian rule as particularly suitable for cathedral churches. While his primary concern may have been with the introduction of continental liturgical observances to cathedral churches, it also meant that the bishop was regarded as the titular head of a monastic community, while a prior was responsible for its routine administration. The monastic community also functioned as the cathedral chapter. A reason why Malachy may have regarded the Augustinian rule as particularly appropriate for cathedral churches was that it would promote canonically valid episcopal elections that would be free from secular pressures and hereditarily entrenched family ties since the electoral body would be made up of the monastic community. Due weight should probably also be accorded to the fact that, in imitation of the *vita apostolica* of the early church, the income or property of the see was to be held in common between bishop and monastic community. This would have precluded the appropriation by the bishop of property pertaining to the see. About 1102 Anselm, archbishop of Canterbury, had written to Samuel Ua hAingliu, bishop of Dublin, complaining that books and vestments which had been given by the church of Canterbury to Samuel's predecessor had not been intended as a personal gift, but for the use of the church of Dublin. Samuel was a nephew of his immediate predecessor, Donatus or Donngus, and Anselm's letter illustrates how privatisation of church property was considered an abuse that impeded the progress of reform. Introducing a community of Augustinian canons to Christ Church Cathedral would have worked against such tendencies.

Together, the Cistercian and Augustinian rules were to effect a radical transformation of the older Irish monasticism and bring it more into line with contemporary continental practices. More doubtful is whether monastic recruits were drawn from a wider spectrum of society than previously. There is little evidence for a dramatic extension of the monastic vocation to include many who would previously not have had the opportunity to become monks. What evidence there is suggests that monastic recruits continued to be drawn primarily from the social elite, from aristocratic and landed families, though the Cistercians, in having both choir monks and brothers, probably did draw men of a lower social status than might otherwise have been accepted into a monastic community.

Another testimony to change in the twelfth-century Irish church was the adoption of what may be termed universal or pan-Christian church dedications. The Irish church had a highly localised repertoire of church dedications. Churches generally were dedicated to their founder: to found a church had automatically conferred saintly status. In the course of the twelfth century the intense regionalism of church dedications that had been a characteristic generally in Europe began to change. As elsewhere in Europe, dedications associated with the Lord, the Virgin Mary and the apostles come to predominate. Thus, the cathedral churches of Dublin, Waterford, and Downpatrick were dedicated to the Holy Trinity, while the cathedral church of Limerick was dedicated to the Virgin Mary (these are not comprehensive lists).

The adoption of these universal or pan-Christian church dedications in Ireland must have stimulated the acquisition of new devotional objects, such as statues and altar furnishings, very little of which, however, alas now remain. The new continental devotion to the crucified humanity of Christ, to the suffering Christ which replaced earlier depictions of Christ in majesty, is reflected in the accounts of the speaking crucifix of Holy Trinity (or Christ Church Cathedral as it later came to be known), to which was attributed miraculous powers. The crucifix was described by one chronicler as especially expressive; in fact, so expressive that in 1197 the crucifix is recorded to have gone into agony, the face of Christ reddening and perspiring, and then even more remarkably, a mixture of blood and water poured from its side; and all because certain property rights of the archbishop of Dublin had been infringed.

Not only the churches, but also Irish churchmen, changed their names, at least when writing in the Latin language. They adopted biblical forenames, both Old and New Testament names, so as to signal their membership of the universal church. Better known to us as St Malachy of Armagh, Malachy's vernacular Irish name was Máel Máedóc, literally the servant of Máedóc, a sixth-century Irish saint associated with the church of Ferns (Co Wexford). Máel Maedóc adopted the name of the Old Testament prophet, Malachias, in Hebrew 'messenger', and it was undoubtedly chosen intentionally to convey to his clerical contemporaries that he had a particular message of reform to preach. Lorcán Ua Tuathail, archbishop of Dublin, styled himself Laurentius in the Latin charters that he issued, perhaps because St Laurence was associated with the church of Rome. All the Irish bishops of the twelfth century used Latinised names. Sometimes, the Latin names may have been chosen for their similarity of sound to Irish forenames. Gillebertus, bishop of Limerick, occurs in vernacular Irish sources as Gille or Gille Espaic. Some undoubtedly were more deliberate. The choice by Gilla Meic Liac, archbishop of Armagh (d. 1174), of the Latin name, Gelasius, was probably intended to convey a contemporary message. Pope Gelasius in the fifth century had played an important role in seeking to define more clearly the separation of church and state. Gilla Meic Liac, in choosing a papal name Gelasius, almost certainly intended to highlight his direct link as primate of the Irish church with the papacy, and to recall that specific attribute of Pope Gelasius, that is, to emphasise the independence of the Irish church from lay interference. Irish clergy, at least when writing in Latin, felt the need to adopt a Christian name that linked them with, and would have been familiar to, their European counterparts. Their sense of belonging to a universal Christian and clerical community is apparent also in the letters that Irish churchmen exchanged with other prominent ecclesiastics, such as the archbishops of Canterbury, or Bernard, abbot of Clairvaux, letters which reflect the friendship networks of the twelfth century, and linked the Irish correspondents into those networks.

Did the new structures and reforming initiatives in the religious life enable the church to engage more effectively with the mass of the faithful and not so faithful? The church in its narrow sense referred to the clergy and the corporate property owning institution of the church, but in a broader sense it included all baptised Christians. The reformation of the Irish church ought to have affected far more than the institutional church and its clergy, but it is difficult to recover information about the impact of the new structures on the laity or their Christian life. How the Christian message was preached to the laity remains largely unknown. Its efficacy would have depended to a large part on the training and standard of education of the parochial clergy. The spiritual understanding of the laity would have been formed orally by preaching and the liturgy and visually through wall paintings, stained glass, and other church furnishings. One area about which there is information relating to the laity is the practice of pilgrimage. Pilgrimage, undertaken for spiritual or physical healing, was central to the religious life of the laity. To the established long distance destinations of Rome and the Holy Land were added newer venues in the twelfth century like Canterbury which became a place of pilgrimage to the shrine of the murdered archbishop, Thomas Becket, after 1170, and Santiago de Compostella in northern Spain. Pilgrimage to these long haul destinations would have been restricted to the wealthy, but there were other more local shrines to hand. Relics might be visited and publicly honoured at a shrine. They might be used not only for liturgical ritual, but also for public oath-swearing ceremonies, as certainly was the case with the speaking crucifix of Christ Church Cathedral, Dublin.

Thus far, the changes that the Irish church underwent in the twelfth century have been presented in more or less neutral terms as a process of Europeanisation. But it was not mere Europeanisation that persuaded contemporaries, both non-Irish and Irish, to promote such vigorous re-organisation within the Irish church. Rather, Europeanisation was conceived of as synonymous with reformation; and there is no doubt that by the twelfth century the Irish church was in need of a reforming impulse to redress an ever increasing tendency towards secularisation that had emerged as a noticeable feature of the post-Viking Irish church. In the early medieval period Irish churchmen had been responsible for inaugurating a spiritual renewal on the continent. Christianity in fifth-century Ireland had had to adapt to the radically different conditions of a non-Romanised and predominantly rural society. Ireland had received a late antique Mediterranean, urban-based, Christianity in the fifth century and it had reinvigorated and adapted that Christianity to the changed conditions of the predominantly rural society of early Ireland. In the late sixth century Irish missionaries like Columbanus had taken that reinvigorated Christianity back to post-Roman Europe, to the now predominantly rural society of early medieval Europe, where they made such a positive impact that the Irish acquired a reputation as saints and scholars. In the twelfth century Ireland's peripheral location had more negative consequences. Change and reform had been initiated at the centre and percolated more slowly to the peripheries of Europe. One important consequence was that twelfth-century Ireland was perceived by outsiders not simply as different, but also as backward, and worse still by some observers, as barbaric. Bernard of Clairvaux, as he describes in his life of St Malachy of Armagh, was horrified by the fact that the headship of the church of Armagh had been controlled by a hereditarily entrenched lay family, eight members of which passed the office not only from uncle to nephew, and brother to brother, but also from father to son for a hundred and forty year period until 1105. He described a 'total breakdown of ecclesiastical discipline, a relaxation of censure, a weakening of the whole religious structure, with the substitution of cruel barbarity for Christian meekness and paganism brought in under the label of Christianity'.[7] It is important to remember that Bernard's principal informant on the Irish church was Malachy of Armagh. No doubt, native Irish clergy were as outspoken as external commentators, because they had become convinced of, and committed to, the need to re-integrate their church into a wider Christendom whose norms were now taken as standard. The movement for change may have been of external inspiration, but it evoked a strong and committed indigenous reformist response. It is important to bear in mind also that Bernard sought to highlight the achievements of Malachy as a reforming bishop in Ireland by emphasising, if not indeed exaggerating, the obstacles that he had had to overcome.

Images of the otherness of the Irish, by comparison with their continental counterparts, first surface in church reform circles in the twelfth century. The chronological coincidence of the percolation of the continental church reform movement and the colonial intrusion of the Anglo-Normans, or the English, into Ireland from 1169 onwards was to further undermine the very positive reputation that Ireland had enjoyed as an island of saints and scholars in the early medieval period. The negative assessments of church reformers, formulated in the interests of promoting reform, were to be accentuated and perpetuated by more stridently negative English commentators on Ireland. Foremost among them was the prolific and colourful author, Gerald of Wales, the principal apologist for Anglo-Norman intervention in Ireland. Gerald wrote a description of Ireland about 1183 in which he sought to portray the Irish as being completely ignorant of the Christian religion. He recounted an anecdote that he supposedly heard from two sailors who were driven off course by a storm and ended up on the western seaboard of Connacht.[8] There, they happened upon two semi-naked locals with long hair down to their waists. The locals asked the sailors whether they could offer them any meat to eat and, on being told that it was Lent, and that the eating of meat during Lent was forbidden, they replied that they had never heard of Lent. When they were asked whether they were baptised Christians they responded that they had as yet heard nothing of Christ; nor did they know anything about the Christian year, nor the months, weeks, nor the days of the week. Such blatant propaganda as this anecdote in justifica- tion of the English conquest of Ireland fuelled a historiographical tradition of the backward and uncivilised Irish that endured into the nineteenth century, and perhaps even beyond. The criticisms of twelfth-century church reformers, both native and foreign, were to provide a basis for the polemical propaganda of English conquest in Ireland. The fact that it proved possible to justify English intervention in Ireland on the grounds of the need for church reform, because continental changes had reached Ireland later and proceeded more slowly, ensured that the earlier Irish reputation for holiness and scholarship was relentlessly disman- tled under the continual strain of incomplete colonial conquest throughout the remainder of the medieval period.

The movement for Europeanisation – one might alternatively term it the homogenisation or universalisation of the Irish church in the twelfth century, or a shift from localism to univer- salism – was the most important watershed between the intro- duction of Christianity into Ireland in the fifth century and the advent of the Protestant Reformation in the sixteenth century. Taking the long-span view of 2000 years of Christianity, the twelfth century was an important turning point in the history of Christianity in Ireland. It is impossible to gauge how the Irish church might have developed without the English intrusion of the late twelfth century. English intervention ensured that Europeanisation of the Irish church was to become Anglicisation in those areas colonised by the Anglo-Normans. Conversely, in the remaining Irish-held areas a process of re-Gaelicisation was to emerge in the later medieval period, which was to result in a church *inter Hibernicos* and *inter Anglicos*.

The twelfth century was the high point in the European-isation of the Irish church in the medieval period, a turning-point in its history, the impact of which is still readily apparent in the many new twelfth-century church buildings that were built or refurbished in the Romanesque or Gothic styles. In the early medieval period the exceptional circumstances of political upheaval consequent on the collapse of the Roman empire and Germanic migrations and settlements had afforded the early Irish church the opportunity of making a significant contribu-tion to early medieval Christianity. From the twelfth century on-wards, however, in a wider European perspective, the Irish church was to be no more than a regional, outlying church that inevitably received developments from the core area of central Europe at a later date and in more attenuated form. This is, of course, a perspective from hindsight. While the higher ranks of the Irish clergy may have been aware of that difference, for the vast majority of the laity of the time what would have mattered was their own personal religious experience. Unfortunately, it is precisely that aspect of the twelfth-century reform movement about which it is most difficult to recover information. We can, however, have some intimation of how the twelfth-century citi-zen of Dublin visiting Christ Church Cathedral would have experienced in a very dramatic way the visual impact of the transformation of the Irish church in the twelfth century which is conventionally, if too narrowly, described as the twelfth-cent-ury reform.

Notes
1. Sheehy, *Pontificia Hibernica*, i, no. 2.
2. Fleming, *Gille of Limerick*, p. 167.
3. Sheehy, *Pontificia Hibernica*, i, no. 23.
4. *Annals of Ulster*, 1028.7.
5. Etchingham, 'Bishops in the early Irish church', pp. 35-62.
6. Fleming, *Gille of Limerick*, pp. 148-9, 158-9.
7. Bernard of Clairvaux, *Life and death of Malachy, the Irishman*, p. 38.
8. Gerald of Wales, *History and topography*, pp. 110-12.

Bibliography
Primary sources:
Annals of Ulster, ed. Seán Mac Airt and Gearóid Mac Niocaill, Dublin Institute for Advanced Studies, Dublin 1983.

Bernard of Clairvaux, *The life and death of St Malachy the Irishman*, translated Robert T. Meyer, Cistercian Publications, Kalamazoo 1978.

Fleming, John, *Gille of Limerick (c.1070-1145): architect of a medieval church*, Four Courts Press, Dublin 2001.

Gerald of Wales, *The history and topography of Ireland*, Penguin, Harmondsworth 1982.

Sheehy, Maurice P., *Pontificia Hibernica: Medieval papal chancery documents concerning Ireland, 640-1261*, Gill, Dublin 1962-5.

Secondary sources:
Etchingham, Colmán, 'Bishops in the early Irish church: a reassessment' in *Studia Hibernica*, 28 (1994), 35-62.

Gwynn, Aubrey, *The Irish church in the eleventh and twelfth centuries*, ed. Gerard O'Brien, Four Courts Press, Dublin 1992.

Henry, Françoise, *Irish art in the Romanesque Period (1020-1170 A.D.)*, Methuen, London 1970.

Kinsella, Stuart, ed., *Augustinians at Christ Church: the canons regular of the cathedral priory of Holy Trinity, Dublin*, Christ Church Publications, Dublin 2000.

Stalley, Roger, *The Cistercian monasteries of Ireland*, Yale University Press, London and New Haven 1987.

— *Architecture and sculpture in Ireland, 1150-1350*, Gill and Macmillan, Dublin 1971.

Watt, John A., *The church in medieval Ireland*, 2nd edn, University College Dublin Press, Dublin 1998.

First delivered under the title 'The twelfth-century reform of the Irish church' on 12 February 2002

Mendicant Orders in Ireland[1]

Bernadette Williams

There were four major mendicant orders:[2] the Order of Friars Minor (Franciscans), founded by St Francis of Assisi; the Order of Preachers (Dominicans), founded by St Dominic; the Carmelites who originated as hermits in Palestine and evolved into an urban mendicant order; and, finally, the Hermits of St Augustine (Augustinians[3]) who also originated as hermits and evolved into a mendicant order. The garments worn by three of the four orders were responsible for additional names: the Franciscans, the Greyfriars; the Dominicans, the Blackfriars and the Carmelites, the Whitefriars.

The mendicant friars were quite revolutionary. They did not fit into the established order of the medieval church; they were religious but they were not monks. The monk lived a contemplative life with his fellow monks in a monastery and isolated from the world. The friar lived with his fellow friars but amidst the hustle and bustle of town life and the very *raison d'être* of his existence was the exercise of public ministry. The monk was bound by a vow of stability that bound him for life to one monastery. The friar belonged to the convent in which he had taken the habit, but he could well be absent from it for the greater part of his life. The monk took a vow of poverty that bound him strictly as an individual but in no way affected the right of his order to hold extensive property. The friar also took a vow of poverty not only as an individual but, in the early period, as a whole order, thus having no fixed revenues and no properties. The friar should exist upon his own labour and, if necessary and freely offered, the voluntary donations of the faithful; hence the term mendicant.

The reason for the rise of the mendicant orders was related to the economic and social changes which began in the eleventh century. These changes gave rise to a new level of spiritual and intellectual awareness, fuelled by lay literacy, in the towns and cities. There was dissatisfaction with the secular clergy and distaste for the very obvious wealth and worldliness of the established church. Bishops were visibly affluent and monks of all orders owned vast property. This great wealth was perceived as having strayed a long way from the ideals of Jesus Christ and his apostles[4] and consequent upon this disillusionment was the growing attraction of heretical sects such as the Cathars. This new development, of looking to alternatives, greatly worried the established church and it was into this climate of heresy and the questioning of the established church that two new orders came into being: the Order of Friars Minor (Franciscans) and the Order of Preachers (Dominicans). The ethos of the Order of Friars Minor was to minister humbly to the people and lead by example whereas preaching and combating heresy was the *raison d'être* of the Order of Preachers.

In 1215 the Fourth Lateran Council, the greatest and most famous of the medieval councils, presided over by Pope Innocent III, met in Rome where a very wide range of topics was discussed, among which were the problem of heresies and the numerous new orders which had sprung into existence in recent years. A decree was passed strictly forbidding the foundation of new orders; those wishing to join the religious life must enter one of the existing approved orders. An exception to this decree was the new Order of Friars Minor founded by the layman, St Francis of Assisi.[5] St Francis from the beginning had placed himself and his friars wholly under the authority of the pope and thus ensured the survival of the order. The pope announced to the council that the Order of Friars Minor was to be regarded as one of the existing orders. Also present at the Lateran council was Dominic de Guzman, a former Augustinian canon and priest, who was there in order to seek confirmation of the Order of Preachers which he had founded, under the auspices of Fulk,

Archbishop of Toulouse. Pope Innocent III persuaded Dominic to follow the Rule of St Augustine, with such additions as were necessary for his particular needs.

The imitation of the apostolic life was the essential element for St Francis and his disciples, who strove to preach the gospel by the example of the quality of their lives. St Francis was particularly inspired by Mt 10:7-9. The premise was that they should possess nothing; they would support themselves by work for which they would receive food and shelter only and, if necessary, they would beg for their subsistence. Humility was a keynote and in this spirit of humility the leader of the order became known as minister – to minister to the people. The name chosen for the small group, *fratres minores* (friars minor), stressed their humility. Disciples were attracted to St Francis and the order grew dramatically. Despite the fact that to be a Franciscan was not an easy matter, as it entailed giving up both wealth and family, disciples flocked to the order, although not always with the approval of their families. When the Franciscan Italian chronicler, Salimbene, joined the order his father complained to both the Holy Roman Emperor and the pope saying that the friars minor had stolen his son away from him. Despite a visit from his father and an attempted kidnapping, Salimbene refused to leave the order, even though he was aware that his father was now left without an heir.[6] In ten years there were five thousand Franciscan friars in the world but, unfortunately, when numbers reach this level, a group inevitably becomes an institution and the problem arose of adapting the high ideals of St Francis to a large organisation. Inevitably conflict surfaced concerning the ideal of poverty. St Francis was persuaded to write new rules, which for the first time allowed the friars to have books and then churches. Scholarship had quickly assumed a degree of importance in the order and the friars quickly gained great fame through their scholarly activity in the universities. The order was changing despite the misgivings of St Francis and shortly before his death in 1226, he wrote his *Testament*, which protested against the tendency in the order to establish permanent houses and the tendency to seek or to accept papal privileges. Four years after his death, Pope Gregory IX declared that the *Testament* was not binding upon St Francis's followers. After the death of St Francis the conflict about the ideal of apostolic poverty threatened to split the order.[7] A compromise was reached which maintained the fiction of absolute poverty by providing for 'spiritual friends' who could own property for the friars and the legal fiction of papal ownership of friars' property.[8] The friars never became great property owners; most of their income was in the form of gifts, legacies, fees for burials and masses for the dead.

The Order of Preachers (Dominicans) was founded in 1215 to combat heresy by preaching.[9] From its inception, the Order of Preachers was a learned order and this is reflected in the name of the head of the order; he is called *magister* (master). Just like the Order of Friars Minor, the Order of Preachers grew successful and the laity began to endow the Dominicans with property and wealth, and by the end of the thirteenth century, they were victims of their own success. For example, originally Dominican statutes had decreed modest and humble houses, which were to have a maximum height of twelve feet and their churches were not to exceed thirty feet. The flood of funds into the order led to the erection of great churches and elaborate conventual buildings.

The Carmelite Order began to emerge as a recognisable order around the end of the twelfth century, when groups of hermits in Palestine began to form themselves into a coherent group. With the collapse of the Latin Kingdom of Jerusalem the newly created order migrated to the west; the order first reached England in 1241 in the wake of a returning crusader. Initially the Carmelites wished to remain contemplative, but in less than ten years they were following the example of the Order of Friars Minor and the Order of Preachers. In 1247 the pope, in answer to the Carmelites' request, changed their rule making them fully mendicant and the approval of the Order by the Second Council of Lyons in 1274 secured its permanent position among the mendicant orders. The Carmelite Friars moved into cities and towns and performed pastoral work and, like the Order of Friars Minor and Order of Preachers, they also became involved in universities.[10]

The origin of the Augustinian Friars was in some respects similar to the origin of the Carmelites. The order grew from groups of hermits living in various parts of Italy. In 1244 Pope Innocent IV gathered them together into an order under the Rule of St Augustine. They were to be exempt from diocesan jurisdiction and authorised to preach and hear confessions. In 1256, Pope Alexander formally constituted them as the Order of Friars Hermits of St Augustine. The Augustinian Friars, like the Carmelites, moved from hermitages into the cities and towns, and similarly followed the Order of Friars Minor and the Order of Preachers into the scholastic world of the universities.[11]

Perhaps inevitably, as the mendicant orders became more successful, there came a slow relaxation in their observance of corporate poverty and by the fourteenth century the crisis over poverty which had threatened to split the Franciscans had spread to the other mendicant orders. Complaints at the general chapters of the Dominicans indicate that ideals were tarnished by success. Later in the Middle Ages, the mendicants were also characterised by revivalist groups within the orders.

These new mendicant orders were not introduced without strong opposition from the secular clergy and also from the universities. Initially bishops welcomed the friars, some bishops even becoming friars,[12] but conflict soon arose. As the friars ministered to the people it was to be expected that they should experience some difficulty in fitting into the existing diocesan framework. They were exempt from the jurisdiction of the bishops, were granted extensive faculties for preaching and hearing confessions, together with the right of burial in their own churches. Such rights had hitherto been reserved to the secular clergy. The friars were very popular with the laity; they acted as confessors, preached great sermons and conducted burials. It was natural that the laity should wish to bestow gifts on them and should desire to be buried in or near these friary churches in order that the friars might say masses for their souls. The result of this was that revenues, previously given to the parish priests who depended for a great part of their income on the offerings of the faithful, were diverted to the friars. Naturally, this resulted in tension with the secular clergy who saw their privileges and, perhaps more importantly, their revenues depleted. The result was that almost every pope of the period issued one or more bulls attempting to regulate the tensions between the secular clergy and the mendicants. As early as 1255 the Master General of the Dominicans ordered his friars to be careful not to provoke the secular clergy and, at the Second Council of Lyons in 1274, the Dominicans and Franciscans drew up, approved by the pope, a ten-point programme designed to ease the tension between the friars and the secular clergy[13] – but without great success.

A second area of tension arose within the universities. The mendicants, especially the Order of Preachers, had almost from the beginning included learned men among their members and the Order of Friars Minor quickly followed suit. The result was that the universities became dominated by the mendicants. The opposition to the mendicants was particularly strong at the University of Paris, where the Dominicans and Franciscans opened their schools. One of the most famous of all medieval quarrels is the one centred on the University of Paris in the 1250s and the famous literary composition, 'The Romance of the Rose',[14] is part of that struggle. From Paris the quarrel spread all over western Christendom and was represented in Ireland by Richard FitzRalph, Archbishop of Armagh, who, in the 1350s, preached against the mendicants and in nine propositions attacked their poverty and their privileges.[15] Treatises for and against the mendicants flourished at this period until Pope Alexander IV settled the question. He stated that the mendicants were to continue as a part of a university and reluctantly universities submitted to the orders of the pope.

The arrival of the friars in Ireland

The Irish church was represented at the crucial Fourth Lateran Council in Rome in 1215 by the four archbishops, fourteen bishops, two bishops-elect and probably the representatives of monastic houses and cathedral chapters.[16] The Fourth Lateran Council must have been alive with discussion concerning the two new mendicant orders, especially as both St Francis and St Dominic were also visiting Rome. Even if the prelates from Ireland did not personally meet the two leaders, they would undoubtedly have joined the inevitable discussion that must have ensued. It follows therefore that when both the Order of Preachers and the Order of Friars Minor eventually arrived in Ireland, the bishops were already familiar with their mission. This may, in part, account for their rapid expansion throughout both the Anglo-Irish and Irish communities. The Order of Preachers arrived in Ireland in 1224 and the Order of Friars Minor around the same date (c. 1224-1231). The Carmelites did not arrive until c. 1271 and the Augustinians about 10 years later. It is most probable that all the mendicant orders came to Ireland from England.

With the coming of the friars to Ireland came a revolutionary new religious life bringing a fresh approach to the people at large and the townspeople in particular. The friars needed to be based in a fairly well populated area as their main livelihood derived from acts of charity, although some financial support also came from the patronage of benefactors. The ability to attract the friars to an area without a great monetary outlay must have been of great assistance to the growth of the order in Ireland. The benefactors of these town friaries are difficult to determine with any degree of certainty, except in a few well-documented cases. The lack of source material hampers research into this area as it does into all research into medieval Ireland.[17] With the mendicant orders it is more accurate to speak of benefactors rather than founders as the friaries could initially consist of merely a room or a building lent to the friars by a local friend or benefactor. We find that every principal Anglo-Irish family was connected, in some form or another, with the mendicant friars. The most clearly documented benefactor was the king of England and the Irish kings also supported the friars. In the early days they used a nearby parish church or chapel for worship and prayer. Naturally, as the size of the community grew,[18] purpose built friaries came into being and, as in the rest of Europe, the friars in Ireland quickly acquired their own churches. We know that the Archbishop of Armagh consecrated the church of the Friars Minor in Athlone in 1241.

The friary building was very much part of town life and indeed was often used for the benefit of the townspeople. In 1290 goods from a ship, worth £200, were stolen from the church of the Friars Minor of Youghal.[19] Corn was stored at, and seized from, the church of the friars minor at Ardfert[20] and the *pontificalia* of the Bishop of Annaghdown was seized from the Friars Minor friary at Claregalway, where presumably it was being stored.[21] The friary could also be used as a meeting place; the Justiciar of Ireland was appointed in the church of the Friars Minor at Trim in 1391[22] and Richard II stayed with the friars of Drogheda in 1394.[23]

The Black Death of 1348 highlights the close relationship that the friars had with the townspeople. The friars were particularly susceptible to the plague as they lived within the towns and ministered to the people; the Franciscan friar, John Clyn of Kilkenny, tells us that in Kilkenny the confessor died with the confessed. He also tells us that in the Franciscan friary of Drogheda twenty-five friars died, in the Franciscan friary in Dublin twenty-three friars died and in Kilkenny eight of the Dominicans died.[24]

There are various early dates given for the arrival of the Order of Friars Minor in Ireland[25] but the probability is that Ireland was colonised from England soon after 1224 and that the order had made such progress that it was possible to create a separate province by about the year 1230.[26] The Irish Franciscans were independent from the beginning. The Scottish and Welsh were always part of the English Franciscan province. It is most

logical and probable that the first friary was in Dublin.[27] The
first surviving evidence for presence of Franciscans in Dublin is
in January 1233 when a grant of royal alms was given to them
for the repair of their church and house and is therefore evidence
for their presence there for some time.[28] From Dublin the
Franciscan friars quickly moved into the major towns throughout the country. Expansion continued and the growth of the
order in Ireland mirrored that of the rest of Europe. The response to the message of St Francis was just as dramatic in
Ireland as in Europe. The experience of Salimbene's father is
mirrored in the reaction of Walter de Burgh, earl of Ulster,
when, in 1258, David, the youngest brother of the earl, joined the
Franciscans in Dublin. The earl objected and his knights, squires
and satellites broke into the church and managed to snatch
him.[28] Salimbene's father was left without an heir; Henry of
Hereford, lord of Otymy in Kildare lost his son and heir to the
Franciscan order, and because of this the inheritance devolved
to the female line.[29]

Both Anglo Irish and Irish bishops were present at the Fourth
Lateran Council of 1215[30] and this might be partly responsible
for the speed at which the Franciscans and Dominicans also
reached the Irish population. Some Franciscan friaries were particularly Irish in origin, namely Buttevant, Armagh, Ennis,
Timolegue, Killeigh and Cavan. Proof of the rapid spread of the
Franciscan message to the Irish population can be seen by the
large number of Irish Franciscans in episcopal appointments.
Between 1244 and 1317 seventeen Franciscan friars were appointed to bishoprics in Ireland and at least ten of those were
clearly Irish.[31]

Initially, it would appear that there was no racial tension in
the order in Ireland. The first hint of racial tension became apparent, however, in 1285 when both the Dominicans and
Franciscans were accused of making much of the Irish language
and way of life. Nicholas de Cusack, the Anglo-Irish Franciscan
bishop of Kildare, wrote to Edward I warning him against
'insolent religious of the Irish tongue' who told the Irish and

their kings that they were justified, by human and divine law, in fighting for their country and attacking the English conquerors. Nicholas de Cusack suggested that the solution might be to remove friars with Irish sympathies from convents in dangerous districts.[32] Racial animosity found expression once again during the Bruce Invasion in 1315-17, when, understandably, itinerant friars were often viewed with suspicion as they could travel among both races with ease and therefore possibly pass sensitive information. In 1316, Edward II sent two English Franciscan friars to the pope with a letter which stated that the Irish Franciscans had incited the Irish laity against the king. In 1317 the pope responded ordering the archbishops of Dublin and Cashel to warn all persons, especially the members of the four mendicant orders, to desist from treasonable practices against the English or be excommunicated.[33] The other side of the story came in 1317 when Donal O'Neill, in his Remonstrance to Pope John XXII, singled out a friar (Simon le Mercer of Drogheda) as a believer in the maxim that it was no more a sin to kill an Irishman than a dog.[34] After the Bruce invasion the situation between the 'two nations' of Franciscans in Ireland did not improve.

In 1325 the Franciscan friar, John Clyn, reported in his annals that there was strife among the friars, based on 'racial preference and prejudice of nation, language, and blood'.[35] The remedy was complete segregation of Irish and Anglo-Irish Franciscan friars and this was approved by the General Chapter of Lyons in 1325. A new custody was now established at Cork which encompassed the houses of Cork, Buttevant, Limerick and Ardfert. These friaries were removed from the control of the Irish and given to the English friars. Nenagh was now the head of a purely Irish custody which consisted of Ennis, Claregalway, Galway, Armagh, Cavan, Killeigh and Athlone, and it is interesting to note that in 1327, royal alms were transferred from the Irish friars at Athlone to the Anglo Irish friars at Cashel.[36]

The Order of Preachers arrived in Ireland at the early date of 1224.[37] Unlike the Order of Friars Minor, they were never an independent order in Ireland but were always part of the English province subject to the English Provincial until 1484.[38] They quickly established themselves in Dublin, Drogheda, Kilkenny, Waterford, Limerick and Cork. These initial six friaries rose to twenty-four by 1291, with five of those being Irish; Irish patronage was also an early aspect of the Dominicans.

The Cistercians of St Mary's were most probably responsible for the establishment of the Order of Preachers in Dublin.[39] St Saviour's priory in Dublin was situated on the north side of the river Liffey and, in 1706, a Dominican historian described it as situated on the banks of the river so that, when the tide was in, ships could come up to its walls. He also tells us that the land had first belonged to the monks of St Bernard (Cistercians) who gave it to the Dominicans on condition that on Christmas day every year the friars should offer a lighted candle to the abbot of St Mary's, in acknowledgement of the gift.[40]

We have some information about the physical appearance of the Dublin church from the annals written by John de Pembridge, prior of the Dominican friary in Dublin in the mid-fourteenth century.[41] The first church was burnt in a fire in June 1304 and, in the following February, Eustace le Poer laid the first stone of the choir. John le Decer, mayor of Dublin, provided one stone buttress in the church and one altar stone for the high altar together with its ornaments in 1308 (incidentally, we are also informed that the friars dined once a week at his table). The Dominican church seems to have been ill fated because, in 1316, when the Scots were approaching, 'the mayor, Robert de Nottingham, and the citizens of Dublin destroyed the church and used the stones to strengthen the city walls.' After the crisis was over, the king ordered Dublin to re-build the convent for the friars just as it had been before. A later mayor, Kendrick Sherman, erected the campanile under which he was buried in 1351; he had also glazed the windows in the chapter choir and roofed the church. A citizen of Dublin, Maurice Doncreff, gave £40 towards the glazing of the church and was buried in the Dominican cemetery there in 1361. The campanile was also unlucky because it was demolished in a great storm in 1361. It is also from Pembridge that we learn the names of the four founding teachers at the newly instituted – albeit abortive – university at Dublin in 1320. We are told that the first master was friar William de Hardits, Order of Preachers, the second was Henry Cogry, Order of Friars Minor, the third was the dean of St Patrick's and the fourth master – in sacred theology – was the friar Edmund de Kermerdyn.[42]

When Pembridge reported the great controversy between Archbishop FitzRalph and the mendicants in 1358 he displayed his bias by stating 'but in the end the friars got the mastery and the pope caused the Archbishop of Armagh to hold his peace'. Two years later he reported the death, in Avignon, of FitzRalph and he tells us that his bones were conveyed to Ireland to be placed in the Church of St Nicholas, Dundalk, where he was born, after which statement, Pembridge added the dismissive rider, 'But it is doubted whether they were his bones or those of some other man.'

A clash between the secular clergy and the mendicants surrounded the beginning of the Dominican friary at Kilmallock in 1291. John Bluet, burgess of Kilmallock, purchased land for the Dominicans but the Bishop of Limerick ordered his men to eject the friars. The king, having been appealed to, ordered an inquisition into the matter 'to know by whom and by whose authority the friars had been expelled'. The inquisition found in favour of the friars.[43] Other friaries were established more peacefully. We are very fortunate in the survival of the *Register of Athenry*, which contains invaluable information on the foundation and building programme of Milo de Bermingham who invited the Dominicans to Athenry. He bought the site for one hundred and sixty marks and gave another hundred and sixty towards the cost of the building. He also persuaded his knights and soldiers to give financial support to the friars. It is from the *Register of Athenry* that we learn the story of the foundation of Strade, in Mayo, which was established in 1252 by Jordan de Exonia. Jordan de Exonia established the friary initially for the

Franciscans – presumably the mendicant order that he and or his family supported. His wife, however, was Basilia de Bermingham, daughter of Milo, the founder of Athenry. She, following her family's support for the Order of Preachers, was determined that Strade should be Dominican. When her father was due to visit she told her husband that she would neither eat nor drink until her request was granted. Her husband gave in and Basilia duly dispatched a messenger to Rome with a large sum of money to facilitate the transfer of the house to the Dominicans.[44]

The Carmelites were in Ireland by 1271.[45] The Irish province was initially part of the English province but the Irish Carmelites soon sought to separate themselves from England and, despite some opposition, by 1305 they had succeeded. All their churches were dedicated to Our Lady except Knocktopher which was dedicated to St Saviour. The first Carmelite friary, Leighlinbridge, county Carlow, is of great interest. It was founded around 1272 by the Carew family. Leighlinbridge was a dangerous place to site any Anglo-Irish establishment at that period situated as it was between the land of peace and the land of war. For the whole medieval period the Carmelite friars maintained the bridge which was an access point for those going and coming on business to Dublin and also provided lodging for the traveller. There were constant pleas to the crown for help to maintain this great burden.[46] At one point the prior, Robert Rowe, complained to the crown that the house had been so plundered by the Irish that the house and adjacent lands were totally destroyed leaving no source of maintenance unless the king, in recognition of their good work, gave alms.[47]

The first safe date for the Carmelite friary in Whitefriars Street in Dublin is 1279 when, as a result of an enquiry, it was stated that the presence of the Carmelites there would raise the tone of the whole area, as previously courtesans had lived there and evildoers had been harboured there.[48] The church was near the Exchequer and anyone coming up to Dublin to pay in their accounts would pass it on their way. In 1316 the chantry of the Exchequer was granted to the Carmelites in return for celebrat-

ing divine service for the Exchequer either in the city or wherever
the Exchequer should be at the time.[49] A yearly stipend of 100
shillings, constantly renewed, was granted for the friars who
were to pray for the royal family.[50] A former treasurer of Ireland
and benefactor, Hugh de Burgh, was buried there in 1352. After
his death an inventory was made of his goods, as he had died in
debt to the crown and his property had to be assessed. The prior,
Robert Serle, was accused of having a very large quantity of silver chalices, cruets, candlesticks etc., property of Hugh de
Burgh. The prior successfully claimed that Hugh, long before his
death, had donated those items to the friary 'for the good of his
soul'.[51]

Familial loyalty to an order (as demonstrated by the de
Berminghams in relation to Strade) may account for the Carmelite
friary in Kildare. The de Vescys had founded a Carmelite friary at
Hulne in the north of England in 1242 and when William de
Vescy became Justiciar of Ireland he installed the Carmelites in
Kildare. The Carmelites are mentioned – together with the
Franciscans – in the famous medieval poem *The Land of Cokayne*,
written at Kildare towards the end of the thirteenth century. A
medieval satirical poem on the religious in Drogheda makes special mention of white 'copes' when speaking of the Carmelites
there.[52] An Irish Carmelite, Ralph Kelly, rose to great heights in
the order, becoming the Procurator General. He was born in
Drogheda. According to John Bale, the English Carmelite historian
of the sixteenth century, Ralph Kelly's father was David O'Buge,
the Carmelite theologian and canonist, and his mother the wife of
a Drogheda merchant. Ralph Kelly was educated in the Carmelite
house at Kildare where he joined the order, and subsequently
studied canon law at Rome and Avignon. Later in life he became
Bishop of Leighlin before becoming Archbishop of Cashel. In
1353, while Ralph Kelly was Archbishop of Cashel, Roger
Craddock, Bishop of Waterford and Lismore, convicted two
Irishmen of heresy and, without seeking permission of his metropolitan, burned them to death. Ralph Kelly marshalled his troops
and attacked and wounded the bishop.[53]

The Augustinian friars, who arrived in Ireland in the last quarter of the thirteenth century, were introduced from England.[54] The first house was founded at Dublin about 1280, and others quickly followed with the usual enthusiasm. The Dublin friary could not have been established before 1275, when Katherine le Grant of Dublin left bequests in her will to the various religious houses in the city, to the Franciscans, Dominicans, Carmelites and Friars of the Sack, but there was no mention of the Augustinians.[55] However, in April 1282 when William de Stafford, prior to his departure for the Holy Land, left legacies to various mendicant churches in Dublin, the Augustinian friars were included.[56]

The Dublin Augustinian friary was situated on the south bank of the Liffey. While the Carmelites said mass in the Exchequer, the Augustinians were appointed to say mass in the castle. From 1354 a payment was being made in perpetuity for celebrating divine service in the chapel of Dublin castle for the health of the king and queen and their children and for the souls of the king's ancestors.[57] The Augustinians, like the other mendicant orders, were enthusiastic educators and in 1348 petitioned the king for financial assistance to send six friars from the Irish houses to study theology and the liberal arts in England because such studies could not be done in Ireland.[58] The Augustinians were not present to any noticeable degree in the Irish areas until the first half of the fifteenth century. They did not establish houses among the Irish or accept Irishmen until the early fifteenth century. There was direct supervision from England until the mid-fourteenth century when the Anglo-Irish friars refused to submit to the adverse decisions of the English Provincial and sent delegates to the General Chapter in 1391, after which there was a limited local self-government which was confirmed in 1394.

A brief mention can be made of Friars of the Sack, the short-lived mendicant order abolished at the Second Council of Lyons in 1274. According to medieval Franciscan annals, the Friars of the Sack entered Ireland in 1268 where they had one foundation only which was in Dublin. They are mentioned in 1275 when Katherine le Grant of Dublin left bequests in her will to the various religious houses in the city and included the Friars of the Sack, and are also mentioned in 1282 by William de Stafford. They were still in existence in 1310 when their church was broken into in Dublin.[59]

The mendicant orders made a significant impact on society – they radically changed the face of parochial life and raised the expectations of the laity in regard to the education and ability of local parish priests; slack and ignorant clergy would no longer be tolerated without question. At the Fourth Lateran Council of 1215, Pope Innocent III stated that its task was 'the reformation of the universal church'. The problems which beset the church had been gaining in momentum and had demonstrated that there was an urgent need for educated and knowledgeable clergy. This need was met by the highly trained mendicant orders. Increasingly popes relied on the friars rather than the secular clergy to institute and carry out their reforms. The mendicants' loyalty was not diffused by the need to placate local authority – as was the seculars. The mendicants' loyalty was to be to the pope – they were outside episcopal and local secular influences.

Notes

1. For an all-purpose account of the mendicants in general, see C. H. Lawrence, *The Friars*, London 1992.

2. There were three other mendicant orders in Ireland: Friars of the Sack who had one house in Dublin in 1268 and were abolished in 1274 by the General Council of Lyons; the Trinitarians who had one house in Adare and the *Fratres Cruciferi* (Crutched friars) who were not mendicant but Hospitallers, see A. Gwynn and R. N. Hadcock, *Medieval Religious Houses: Ireland*, London 1970, p. 208-9.

3. Known as Austin friars in England.

4. The twelfth century reformer, Arnold of Brescia, went so far as to state that monks and clerics who possessed property or exercised secular power could not be saved.

5. A good general guide is J. R. H. Moorman, *A History of the Franciscan Order from its Origins to the Year 1517*, Oxford 1968; also valuable is Duncan Nimmo, *Franciscan Order: from St Francis to the Foundation of the Capuchins*, Rome 1987. There are numerous histories of St Francis, for

example, J. R. H. Moorman, *St Francis of Assisi*, London 1976.

6. *Chronicle of Salimbene de Adam*, eds. Joseph L. Baird, Guiseppe Baglivi and John Robert Kane, New York 1986, p 13.

7. M. D. Lambert, 'The Franciscan Crisis under John XXII', *Franciscan Studies* 32 (1972) pp. 123-43.

8. Moorman, *History*, pp. 116-7.

9. For a history of the Dominican order see, W. A. Hinnesbusch, OP, *History of the Dominican Order, Origins and Growth to 1550*, 2 vols., New York 1965. For an account of St Dominic and the foundation of the order see M. H. Vicaire, *St Dominic and his Times*, transl. K. Pond, 1964.

10. For a recent account see A. Jotischky, *The Carmelites and Antiquity: Mendicants and their Pasts in the Middle Ages*, Oxford 2002.

11. F. Roth, *The English Austin Friars*, 2 vols., New York 1961.

12. Episcopal wills also give evidence of support for the friars in the thirteenth century, J. R. H. Moorman, *Church Life in England in the Thirteenth Century*, Cambridge 1946, pp. 370-1. The archdeacon of Cloyne was buried in the habit of the Friars Minor in 1271, *Annals of Inisfallen*, ed. Seán Mac Airt, Dublin 1951, p. 369.

13. R. W. Emery, 'Second Council of Lyons', *Catholic Historical Review* 39 (1953), p. 260.

14. There are many editions of this medieval text, for example, *The Romance of the Rose*, Oxford World's Classics, Guillaume de Lorris, Jean de Meun, ed. and transl. Frances Horgan, Oxford 1999.

15. For a comprehensive account of Archbishop FitzRalph see, K. Walsh, *A Fourteenth Century Scholar and Primate: Richard FitzRalph in Oxford, Avignon and Armagh*, Oxford 1981. For a more specific treatment of the problem see J. Coleman, 'FitzRalph's antimendicant "proposicio" (1350) and the politics of the papal court at Avignon', *Journal of Ecclesiastical History* 35 (1984), pp. 376-390.

16. P. J. Dunning, 'Irish Representatives and Irish Ecclesiastical Affairs at the Fourth Lateran Council', *Medieval Studies Presented to Aubrey Gwynn, SJ*, eds., J. A. Watt, J. B. Morrall and F. X. Martin, OSA, Dublin 1961, p 91.

17. The history of individual mendicant friaries throughout this period can only be gleaned by a trawl through the extant medieval documents, many still in manuscript form or edited in record print and Latin.

18. The size of individual friaries at any point in time is difficult to determine; perhaps 15-16 friars per house in 1254, E. Bolster, *A History of the Diocese of Cork*, Shannon 1972, p. 212.

19. *Calendar of Documents relating to Ireland, 1285-1292*, ed. H. S. Sweetman, London 1879, p. 320.

20. A. G. Little and J. E. Fitzmaurice, *Materials for the History of the Franciscan Province of Ireland, A.D. 1230-1450*, Manchester 1920, p. 86.

21. ibid., p 70, 73-4, 79.

22. ibid., p. 166.

23. ibid., p. 167. E. Curtis, *Richard II in Ireland, 1394-5, and Submissions of the Irish Chiefs,* Oxford 1927, p. 37.

24. *Annals of Ireland by Friar John Clyn and Thady Dowling, together with the Annals of Ross,* ed. R. Butler, Ir. Arch. Soc., Dublin 1849, pp. 35-37.

25. For the Franciscans in Ireland, see Francis Cotter, OFM, *The Friars Minor in Ireland from their Arrival to 1400,* New York 1994. For a documented history, see A. G. Little and J. E. Fitzmaurice, *Materials for the History of the Franciscan Province of Ireland, A.D. 1230-1450,* Manchester 1920. For the later Observant Friars, see Colmán N. Ó Clabaigh, OSB, *The Franciscans in Ireland, 1400-1534,* Dublin 2002.

26. Cotter, *The Friars Minor,* p. 11-14.

27. Historically, Youghal was claimed as the first Franciscan friary, ibid pp. 14-17

28. *Liber exemplorum ad usum praedicantium saeculo xiii compositus a quodam fratre minore Anglico de Provincia Hiberniae,* ed. A. G. Little. Aberdeen 1908, pp. 69, 146-7, n117. For a similar incident see G. R. Owst, 'Some Franciscan Memorials at Gray's Inn', *Dublin Review,* (1925), pp. 282-4.

29. *Register of the Abbey of St Thomas, Dublin,* ed. J. T. Gilbert, R. S. London 1889, p. 104.

30. '1215 Conar O'Heney, Bishop of Killaloe, died on his return from the fourth General Council of Lateran', *Annals of the Kingdom of Ireland by the Four Masters, from the earliest period to the year 1616,* ed. J. O'Donovan, vol. 3 , Dublin 1851: reprint, 1991, p. 185.

31. W. R. Thompson, *Friars in the Cathedral: First Franciscan Bishops 1226-1261,* Pontifical Institute of Medieval Studies, Studies and Texts, 33 Toronto 1975, pp. 137-48, 221.

32. Cotter, *Friars Minor,* p. 32-33.

33. ibid., 40-43.

34. E. Curtis and R. B. McDowell, eds., *Irish Historical Documents 1172-1922,* London1943, pp. 38-46.

35. *Annals of Clyn,* p. 17.

36. Fitzmaurice and Little, *Franciscan Province Ire.,* p 129.

37. For the Dominicans in Ireland see D. D. Mould, *The Irish Dominicans,* Dublin 1957; Benedict O' Sullivan, 'The Dominicans in Medieval Ireland', *Medieval Dublin, the living city,* ed. H. Clark, Dublin 1990, pp. 83-99; for the later Dominicans see T. S. Flynn, *The Irish Dominicans 1536-1641,* Dublin 1993. For a valuable early account, see J. O'Heyne, *Epilogus Chronologicus exponens succinte Conventus et Fundationes Sacri Ordinis Praedicatorum in Regno Hyberniae,* Louvain 1760; ed and trans by Ambrose Coleman as *The Irish Dominicans of the Seventeenth Century* together with Ambrose Coleman, *Ancient Dominican Foundations in Ireland,* Dundalk 1902.

38. Gwynn and Hadcock, *Medieval Religious Houses: Ireland,* pp. 218-9. Mould, Irish Dominicans, p. 71.

39. Both William Marshal and Maurice FitzGerald, (both benefactors of the order) are mentioned in connection with bringing the first Friars Preachers to Dublin but without sound supporting documentary evidence. Henry of London, Archbishop of Dublin, has also been proposed but the adverse comment about him by the Dominican Pembridge suggests otherwise, *Chartularies of St Mary's Abbey, Dublin: with the register of its house at Dunbrody, and annals of Ireland*, ed. J. T. Gilbert, vol. 2, R. S. London 1884, p.312.

40. J. O'Heyne and Coleman, p. 25-7

41. All the following information from Pembridge can be found, under the named year in *Chartularies of St Mary's Abbey, Dublin*, vol.2, pp. 303-398.

42. For identification of friar Edmund as a Dominican, Fitzmaurice and Little, see *Franciscan Province Ire.*, p. 108 n.1.

43. *Calendar of Documents 1285-1292*, London 1879, no. 967 (pp. 439-40).

44. 'Regestum monasterii fratrum praedicatorum de Athenry', ed. Ambrose Coleman, *Archivium Hibernica*, 1 (1912), pp. 201-21.

45. For the Carmelites in Ireland, see Peter O'Dwyer, O Carm, *The Irish Carmelites*, Dublin 1988; Peter O'Dwyer, O Carm, 'The Carmelite Order in Pre-Reformation Ireland', *IER*, 110 (1968), pp. 350-63,

46. *Rotulorum patentium et clausorum cancellariae Hiberniae calendarium*, ed. E Tresham, Dublin 1828, 99/6, 103/24, 203/20, 206/123.

47. Philomena Connolly, *Irish Exchequer Payments 1270-1446*, Dublin 1998, pp. 427, 507, 532, 535, 538.

48. *Calendar of Documents relating to Ireland 1252-1284*, London 1877, no. 1609 (p. 332).

49. Tresham, pp. 251/27, 253/3.

50. ibid., pp. 202/28, 206/123, 251/27, 235/3, 240/25, 243/23, 246/24.

51. I am indebted to Dr Philomena Connolly for this information, NAI, RC 8/26 pp.106-9.

52. Fitzmaurice and Little, *Franciscan Province Ire.*, p. 121.

53. D. Gleeson, 'A Fourteenth Century Clare Heresy Trial', *Irish Ecclesiastical Record*, 5th ser., 89 (1958), pp. 36-42.

54. For the Augustinian Friars, see F. X. Martin, 'The Augustinian Friars in Pre-Reformation Ireland', *Augustiniana*, 6 (1956), pp. 346-84.

55. *Christ Church Deeds*, ed M. J. McEnery and Raymond Refaussé, Dublin 2001, p. 54 no. 106.

56. 'Liber Albus of Christ Church, Dublin', ed. H. J. Lawlor, in *Royal Irish Academy Proceedings*, Sec. C. xxvii (1908-9), p. 31.

57. Connolly, *Irish Exchequer Payments*, pp. 475, 489, 503, 508, 510, 513, 525, 526, 532.

58. M. V. Ronan, *The Reformation in Dublin*, London 1926, pp. 203-4.

59. *Calendar of the Justiciary Rolls of Ireland*, ed. Herbert Wood and A. E. Langman; revised by M. C. Griffith, PROI, Dublin 1956, p. 150.

Printed Primary Sources

Annals of Inisfallen, ed. Seán Mac Airt, Dublin 1951, p. 369.

Annals of Ireland by Friar John Clyn and Thady Dowling, together with the Annals of Ross, ed. R. Butler, Ir. Arch. Soc., Dublin1849.

Annals of the Kingdom of Ireland by the Four Masters, ed. J. O'Donovan, 7 vols., Dublin 1851; repr. 1990.

Calendar of Documents relating to Ireland, 1171-1307, ed. H. S. Sweetman, 5 vols., London 1875-86.

Calendar of the Justiciary Rolls, ed. J. Mills, M. C. Griffith, 3 vols., Dublin 1905, 1914,1956.

Chartularies of St Mary's Abbey, Dublin: with the register of its house at Dunbrody, and Annals of Ireland, ed. J. T. Gilbert, 2 vols, R. S. London 1884

Christ Church Deeds, ed M. J. McEnery and Raymond Refaussé, Dublin 2001.

Chronicle of Salimbene de Adam, eds. Joseph L. Baird, Guiseppe Baglivi and John Robert Kane, New York 1986.

Irish Historical Documents 1172-1922, ed. E. Curtis and R. B. McDowell, London 1943.

'Liber Albus of Christ Church, Dublin', ed. H. J. Lawlor, in *Royal Irish Academy Proceedings*, Sec. C. xxvii (1908-9).

Liber exemplorum ad usum praedicantium saeculo xiii compositus a quodam fratre minore Anglico de Provincia Hiberniae, ed. A. G. Little, Aberdeen 1908.

'Regestum monasterii fratrum praedicatorum de Athenry', ed. Ambrose Coleman, *Archivium Hibernica*, 1 (1912), pp. 201-21.

Register of the Abbey of St Thomas the Martyr, Dublin, ed. J. T. Gilbert, R. S. London 1889.

Rotulorum patentium et clausorum cancellariae Hiberniae calendarium, ed. E Tresham, Dublin 1828

The Romance of the Rose, Oxford World's Classics, Guillaume de Lorris, Jean de Meun, ed. and transl. Frances Horgan, Oxford 1999.

Secondary Sources

Bolster, E., *A History of the Diocese of Cork*, Shannon 1972.

Coleman, J., 'FitzRalph's antimendicant "proposicio" (1350) and the politics of the papal court at Avignon', *Journal of Ecclesiastical History*, 35 (1984), pp. 376-390.

Connolly, Philomena, *Irish Exchequer Payments 1270-1446*, Dublin 1998.

Cotter, Francis, OFM, *The Friars Minor in Ireland from their Arrival to 1400*, New York 1994.

Curtis, E., *Richard II in Ireland, 1394-5, and Submissions of the Irish Chiefs*, Oxford 1927.

Dunning, P. J., 'Irish Representatives and Irish Ecclesiastical Affairs at the Fourth Lateran Council', *Medieval Studies Presented to Aubrey Gwynn, SJ*, eds., J. A. Watt, J. B. Morrall and F. X. Martin, OSA,

Dublin 1961, pp. 90-113.

Emery, R. W., 'Second Council of Lyons', *Catholic Historical Review*, 39 (1953), pp 257-271.

Flynn, T. S., *The Irish Dominicans 1536-1641*, Dublin 1993.

Gleeson, D., 'A Fourteenth Century Clare Heresy Trial', *Irish Ecclesiastical Record*, 5th ser., 89 (1958), pp. 36-42.

Gwynn, A. and R. N. Hadcock, *Medieval Religious Houses: Ireland*, London 1970.

Hinnesbusch, W. A. OP, *History of the Dominican Order, Origins and Growth to 1550*, 2 vols., New York 1965.

Jotischky, A., *The Carmelites and Antiquity: Mendicants and their Pasts in the Middle Ages*, Oxford 2002

Lambert, M. D., 'The Franciscan Crisis under John XXII', *Franciscan Studies* 32 (1972) pp. 123-43.

Lawrence, C. H., *The Friars*, London 1992.

Little A. G., and J. E. Fitzmaurice, *Materials for the History of the Franciscan Province of Ireland, A.D. 1230-1450*, Manchester1920.

Martin, F. X., 'The Augustinian Friars in Pre-Reformation Ireland', *Augustiniana*, 6 (1956), pp. 346-84.

Moorman, J. R. H., *A History of the Franciscan Order from its Origins to the Year 1517*, Oxford 1968.

Moorman, J. R. H., *Church Life in England in the Thirteenth Century*, Cambridge 1946.

Moorman, J. R. H., *St Francis of Assisi*, London 1976.

Mould, D. D., *The Irish Dominicans*, Dublin 1957.

Nimmo, Duncan, *Franciscan Order: from St Francis to the Foundation of the Capuchins*, Rome 1987.

Ó Clabaigh, Colmán N., OSB, *The Franciscans in Ireland, 1400-1534*, Dublin 2002.

O'Sullivan, Benedict, 'The Dominicans in medieval Ireland', in *Medieval Dublin, the living city*, ed. H. Clark, Dublin 1990, pp. 83-99.

O'Dwyer, Peter O Carm, *The Irish Carmelites*, Dublin 1988.

O'Dwyer, Peter O Carm, 'The Carmelite Order in Pre-Reformation Ireland', *IER*, 110 (1968), pp. 350-63

O'Heyne, J., *Epilogus Chronologicus exponens succinte Conventus et Fundationes Sacri Ordinis Praedicatorum in Regno Hyberniae*, Louvain 1760; ed and trans, by Ambrose Coleman as *The Irish Dominicans of the Seventeenth Century* together with Ambrose Coleman, *Ancient Dominican Foundations in Ireland*, Dundalk 1902.

Owst, G. R., 'Some Franciscan Memorials at Gray's Inn', *Dublin Review*, 1925.

Ronan, M. V., *The Reformation in Dublin*, London 1926, pp. 203-4.

Roth, F., *The English Austin Friars*, 2 vols., New York 1961.

Thompson, W. R., *Friars in the Cathedral: First Franciscan Bishops 1226-1261*, Pontifical Institute of Medieval Studies, Studies and Texts, 33 Toronto 1975.

Vicaire, M. H., *St Dominic and his Times*, transl. K. Pond, 1964.

Walsh, K., *A Fourteenth Century Scholar and Primate: Richard FitzRalph in Oxford, Avignon and Armagh*, Oxford 1981.

Watt, J. A., *The Church and Two Nations in Medieval Ireland*, Cambridge 1970

First delivered under the title 'The mendicants and the Anglo-Norman church' on 19 February 2002

The Dawn of the Reformation in Ireland

Colm Lennon

The Reformation originated in German-speaking lands in the second and third decades of the sixteenth century mainly as a popular response to vigorous criticism of the Christian church from within the ranks of its intelligentsia. A number of grievances combined to fuel the swelling campaign of protest against aspects of the contemporary practice of Christianity. The quality of ecclesiastical leadership being provided by the popes and senior clerics was a long-standing source of complaint, as was the standard of ministry being exercised by many priests at local level. To clerical worldliness was attributed the spurious application of spiritual benefits, including the preaching of indulgences which drew the ire of Martin Luther. His analysis of the ills of the system eventually issued forth in his critique of the orthodox theory of grace and its role in salvation. Emboldened by the support of some fellow-theologians, he went public with a series of publications that elicited a wave of popular sympathy from Germans, and later natives of other lands. His breaking with the pope and his defiance of the Holy Roman Emperor were sustained by this popularity, but ultimately his establishment of an alternative to the Catholic mode of ecclesial organisation depended upon the backing of secular princes and urban magistracies.

The spread of the Reformation was facilitated by the presence of preconditions for change in the regions that were affected. Not only were there religious sensibilities at work in respect of anti-clericalism and anti-papalism, but also the intellectual milieu favoured change. The Christian humanist emphasis on a return to the springs of pristine Christianity, reflected in the writings of early church figures newly edited for the printing press, imbued many with a thirst for reform. The expansion of political ambition on the part of the dynastic rulers of the early sixteenth century provided an incentive for a change in the system of ecclesiastical rule, or at least the imposition of state power over the church. Economic and social changes in cities and rural communities brought about new attitudes to the exercise of clerical influence and the assertion of clerical privilege. Well before 1517, the year of Luther's protest against indulgences, movements for reform of the institution of the church on the part of the humanists received the approval of secular rulers who saw opportunities for self-aggrandisement in the curtailment of clerical and papal power. While much of the reforming effort was directed at change from within, as in the case of Erasmian humanism, Luther was impelled to break with existing structures due to the mishandling by the Roman authorities of the crisis created by his protest, and the encouragement that he got for his Protestantism from many quarters in Germany, clerical and lay, popular and elite.

In England, the Reformation did not at least initially take the form of a movement of popular opposition to the institution of the church. It was not that anti-clerical feelings were necessarily absent there or that hostility to the papacy was non-existent. Moreover, Christian humanism had developed in England from the late fifteenth century, Erasmus, for example, being attracted as a welcome visitor to the country. Recent historical research has shown that by and large the English church at the end of the middle ages was in fairly good condition, and that parish life was flourishing and vibrant on the eve of the Reformation. Anti-clerical attitudes were generally contained within the discourse of theologians and lawyers, and the monarchy had asserted its rights *vis-à-vis* the papacy during the late medieval centuries. The residual heterodoxy of Lollardy, stemming from the reform movement of John Wycliffe, had a few scattered centres of support, mostly in the south of the country. King Henry VIII was to the fore in resisting the campaign of Luther against the salvation

theory of the medieval church and even orchestrated a pam-
phleteering response for which he gained the title *Defensor Fidei*,
or Defender of Faith, from the pope. The king's great matter of the
setting aside of the marriage to Katharine of Aragon, however,
ignited the dispute with the Vatican which eventually led to
Henry's break with Rome and his assumption of the title of
supreme head of the church for himself. Part of the process of
enlisting support for his schismatic campaign entailed foment-
ing public anger against the excesses of clerical power and the
wealth of the monastic orders in England and Wales. But the
early Reformation in England did not officially witness theological innovation and there was fairly limited liturgical change.

Ireland experienced the Reformation by extension from
England. As in England, there was no great protest movement
in being against the church as an institution. In the western island, however, conditions were comparatively different in that
the church was effectively divided into the two zones of '*ecclesia
inter Anglicos*' and '*ecclesia inter Hibernicos*'. In the former, parish
and diocesan life functioned in a very similar way to its counterpart in England, with little manifestation of anti-clericalism or
anti-papalism. In the Gaelic church, institutional life was very
different with a largely hereditary clergy presiding over large
rural parishes and deaneries. A notable feature of this milieu
was the upsurge of observant mendicantism since the mid-fif-
teenth century that saw the foundation of dozens of friaries and
houses of lay tertiaries under the auspices of orders such as
Franciscans. That the Reformation was interpolated into such an
ecclesiastical landscape had more to do with politics than with
religion. Henry VIII was in the process of centralising English
government control in Dublin in the aftermath of the fall of the
Kildare Geraldines in the 1530s, and part of his campaign of asserting his sovereignty over those regions of the island under
English control was the replicating of the church settlement already in place in England.

In 1536, the Irish church was formally detached from Rome
by act of parliament and the king became its supreme head. A

series of other laws of the same assembly gave juridical shape to a church of Ireland, having as its authority source the king of England (as lord of Ireland). Powers of taxation and legal adjudication formerly vested in the Roman curia in respect of the church were now subsumed within an ecclesiastical framework centred on the Irish church (embodied very much in the form of the two archbishops of Dublin and Armagh). To that end, the Englishman, George Browne, a former Augustinian friar, was appointed to the vacant archiepiscopal see of Dublin, the incumbent primate and archbishop of Armagh, George Cromer, apparently opting out of the reform programme. Various penalties were enshrined within the Reformation legislation, enforcing the king's supremacy among clergy and laity. Liturgical change was, however, minimal, with plans for an English-language bible for parish churches being canvassed, and prayers for the king as head of the church supplanting the traditional biddings at the offertory of the mass. As in England, the monasteries within the English sphere of governance were suppressed in the late 1530s and their properties secularised. A systematic visitation of the religious houses resulted in the resignation of the heads and communities (who were pensioned off) and the confiscation of their real estate and chattels. One of the casualties of this campaign was the religious house of canons at Holy Trinity priory, though the institution of Christ Church Cathedral was preserved from dissolution through the pleas of the citizenry of Dublin. In a further extension of the campaign to extirpate perceived excesses of zeal in late medieval spirituality, royal commissioners conducted a campaign of closure of shrines and centres of popular cults and pilgrimages.

Within the sphere of influence of the English administration in Ireland, that is most of Leinster and Munster, in which attempts at enforcing the early Reformation measures were made, the level of acceptance of innovation varied. The secular elite of aristocracy and gentry was not averse to acknowledging Henry VIII as head of the church, being inured in the habit of obedience to the crown. Once their landholding and commercial perquisites

in respect of the monastic sector were assured through negoti-
ation, they viewed the dissolution of the religious orders with
equanimity, benefiting by the dispersal of properties and also
rights to tithes and advowsons. Accordingly a formidable sup-
port-group for a key aspect of change was brought into being.
Among senior clergy, the responses were more mixed. While the
leading bishops within the Englishry came to terms with the
transfer of authority to the king, the diocesan administrators in
Dublin especially were loath to relinquish their traditional privileges in respect of church governance, now threatened under the
new regime. A significant wave of recalcitrance met Archbishop
Browne's visitational and liturgical ventures, not helped by the
reluctance of the secular officials such as Lord Deputy Grey to
weigh in behind the enforcement of the early Reformation.
Lesser clergy demonstrated unease through the proctors, their
representatives in parliament in 1536-7, who for their pains were
excluded from the assembly thereafter. Within the parishes, the
signs of religious change were minimal, the acceptance of new
liturgical practices being very dependent on the predilection of
the parochial clergy. There were some changes in terms of
chapels attached to monasteries and friaries which had communal and cantuarial significance, but by and large parish life continued unaffected during the early phase of Henrician reform.

After the first flush of reform, a veritable moratorium ensued
during the final seven years of Henry VIII's reign. With the promulgation of the conservative Act of Six Articles, the initial
phase of religious innovation was over and consolidation of the
royal supremacy was paramount in Ireland. In the 1540s, the
pacific political climate that obtained under Lord Deputy St
Leger was matched in the ecclesiastical sphere. He oversaw the
extension of royal jurisdiction into Gaelic areas, ensuring that
chieftains who came to terms with Henry's regime under surrender and regrant accepted the king's supremacy also. Some
papally-appointed bishops were similarly offered, and accepted,
the opportunity to surrender their Roman warrants in return for
episcopal credentials granted by the crown. As the royal admin-

istration reached out gradually into western areas, more religious houses were suppressed and their lands granted mostly to local ruling elites to copperfasten support for the political reforms. In this sense, the period was marked by the ascendancy of secular concerns above those of religion. Archbishop Browne's proactive campaign ceased after 1540, vitiated to a large extent by the demise of his English patron, Thomas Cromwell. Instead, church leadership was resumed by a conservative native group, which concentrated on upholding the *status quo*. Only among the observant mendicant orders, especially the Franciscans in the borders between the Pale and the Gaelic areas, was there organised and systematic opposition to the king's taking over of supreme authority within the church in Ireland.

While Henry VIII lived, Protestantism was officially proscribed, but on his death, the reformed religion was introduced, first in England and eventually in Ireland, under the new king, Edward VI, who had been educated by Protestant tutors. Under his rule, the central liturgy of worship, the mass, was substantially changed in line with Protestant thinking, and the iconography of the old church was progressively overturned. Doctrinal reforms were embodied in the first and second *Book of Common Prayer*, promulgated successively in 1549 and 1552. The remaining vestiges of late medieval corporate Christianity were removed when the English chantries and fraternities were suppressed by parliament, the lands and properties becoming part of the bank of secularised real estate for distribution to royal supporters. The imperative of uniformity dictated that the ecclesiastical changes would be applied in Ireland, but no parliament was assembled to ratify the programme. Instead, the introduction of Protestantism in Ireland was to take effect through the proclamations of the chief governor. Significantly, however, the Irish chantries and religious fraternities were left untouched under the Edwardian Reformation, and they survived to become rallying-forces for recusancy at the end of the Tudor period. While Sir Anthony St Leger continued to favour an emollient approach, the lord deputies who interspersed his tenures (until

1548 and again from 1550-1), Sir Edward Bellingham (1548-9) and Sir James Croft (1551-3), were more intent on enforcing conformity. As testimony to St Leger's irenicism, he aspired to the production of an Irish language version of the *Book of Common Prayer* for promoting the changes among the Gaelic-speaking population of the island.

As an adjunct to the Edwardian Reformation, the printing press was introduced into Ireland in 1551. Its first imprint was an English version of the *Book of the Common Prayer*, an indication of the anglocentric nature of the proposed reform. Even within the Englishry, however, there was notable resistance to the reforms in religion. After an energetic start, Archbishop Browne once again experienced the frustration of opposition from his senior clergy who were discommoded by the reduction of St Patrick's, Dublin, from the status of cathedral to that of parish church. In Meath, Bishop Edward Staples's attempts to introduce the reformed liturgy and doctrines elicited serious hostility from the influential gentry class whose patronage within the church was a crucial factor. More significant, perhaps, was the reluctance of the archbishop of Armagh, George Dowdall, to go along with the changes. After the failure of Lord Deputy St Leger to reconcile him to the Protestant order, Dowdall eventually withdrew to the continent, opting out of the Reformation. The most determined attempt to advance the reform in Ireland took place with the appointment of the evangelistic John Bale to the bishopric of Ossory under Croft's deputyship. Bale announced his commitment to the reform by insisting on ordination according to the rites of the more radical second *Book of Common Prayer*. His reception in Kilkenny in 1552 was more or less uniformly hostile among the city's authorities, although he reported that he won some youthful supporters. After several months of discomfiture, Bale was forced to leave his diocese when the death of King Edward in March 1553 paved the way for the accession of the Catholic monarch, Queen Mary.

Under Mary, papal supremacy was restored in both English and Irish churches, and the full panoply of Catholic worship re-instated. The monasteries were not restored to their former owners, however, but in Dublin, St Patrick's was given back its cathedral status. Archbishop Dowdall's return to Armagh symbolised the reconstitution of the old church, and across the clerical leadership in general a reversion to the old worship and beliefs was apparently welcomed. The small community of Protestants in Ireland either withdrew from the country to the continent or else conformed outwardly to the restoration of Catholicism. There were no persecutions of reformed Christians as happened in Mary's England. Overall, there was no reformation of religious life that touched the generality of parishes throughout the country, either under the auspices of the Protestantism of Edward or the Catholicism of Mary. The situation on the ground was naturally confused, given all the changes but, apart from the dissolution of local monasteries and friaries in about half of the country, Christian men and women would have noticed little enough substantial change down to 1560.

The platform for a sustained reformation was laid in that year with the promulgation of the Elizabethan settlement in the form of the parliamentary acts of supremacy and uniformity. Queen Elizabeth I was affirmed as the supreme governor of the Church of Ireland, which was now the state church, established by law, to which all of the queen's subjects were required to belong. Under the act of uniformity, all were enjoined to attend church service according to the rite prescribed by the *Book of Common Prayer*, under penalty of fines. The tenor of the book adopted under Elizabeth was that of moderate Protestantism, and new bodies for the enforcement of discipline among clergy and laity were put in place. In general, the Anglican church took over the existing institution as a going concern. As a concession to socio-cultural conditions in Ireland, licence was given for the *Book of Common Prayer* to be circulated in Latin in areas where English was not understood. While this compromise was a recognition of the reality that the majority of the island's population were Gaelic-speaking, such a dilution of the essential spirit of the Reformation (which was premised on the priesthood of all believers absorbing the gospel for themselves through their vernacular) represented an ominous gulf between the theory and the reality of a Protestant state in Ireland.

As the later Tudor government in Ireland attempted to reach into all of the provinces, a pan-insular Anglican church became at least a possibility. Yet the severe structural problems bedevilling the spread of the Reformation were closely related to the lack of prioritisation of religious reform on the part of the state arm. Even had sufficient ecclesiastical resources allowed for a national campaign of evangelisation to spread the gospel in accordance with the principles of the reformed church, the aims of government policy privileged social and political reform, at times to the detriment of the preaching of the word. In terms of institutional weakness, the chronic under-funding of the bulk of benefices within the church militated against the recruitment of pastors of requisite quality to preach and teach, and also against the erection of schools and ultimately a university, for the education of the laity and a trained ministry. Only within a small minority of dioceses were there sufficiently well-endowed livings to attract clergy of a high calibre from England to take up senior leadership roles. Even within the English Pale, the diocese of Meath, which was ruled by Hugh Brady, a native bishop, in the early Elizabethan period, the poverty of most parishes ensured that only unreformed clergy attached to the old order were prepared to work there as pastors. Many of these were native Irish speakers, ministering to essentially Gaelic-speaking parishioners and thus interposing themselves between the people and the English Reformation. Moreover, the dearth of educational facilities in most dioceses meant that schooling within the reformed milieu was unavailable for young people with the potential to serve the Church of Ireland, and not until 1592 was a native university founded to train a native pastorate equipped to minister in the Irish parishes. A parliamentary initiative for the establishment of diocesan grammar schools in 1570 foundered largely on the reluctance of the impecunious bishops to commit scarce resources to academic projects.

The question of government priorities arises in respect of the application of resources. There is no doubt that most governors in the later sixteenth century period were more anxious to extend secular government into the Irish provinces than to commit funds towards the bolstering of the Irish church. This tied in with the overall thrust of the policy of the anglicisation of the island. The Reformation was to be part of a general transformation of the population into English-speaking subjects who would eventually worship in the Anglican mode. Some proponents of the Reformation in Ireland, of Irish and English birth, desired the acculturation of the religious changes in the native idiom. At Queen Elizabeth's initiative, a Gaelic language printing-press was established in Dublin with the aim of producing an Irish version of the scriptures to underpin the evangelisation of the majority of the people. But, aside from a primer printed under the patronage of the small urban Protestant patriciate in 1571, no major work issued from the press before 1600, thus stunting the efforts of those such as Bishop Brady who envisaged preaching to the Irish-speaking portion of the population in their vernacular. Instead, the official ideology that took root (encompassing the new university on its foundation) stressed the essential Englishness of the Reformation to be preached in the country, and thereby ensured that the religious campaign would be an adjunct to the secular thrust of anglicisation. The perceived unpopularity of the latter policy, especially in its colonial manifestations, damaged the chances of the Reformation being looked upon favourably, at least in the crucial early decades after the Elizabethan settlement.

The parochial clergy that the Church of Ireland took over in 1560 were extremely mixed in terms of backgrounds and outlook. They ranged from the priests of mainly English descent 'inter Anglicos' to the hereditary erenaghs of the church among the Gaelic. While the Anglican authorities wished ultimately to create a new parish ministry, they were compelled to carry on with the inherited incumbents. Most of the 'native' ministry or indigenous clergy succeeded in providing a continuous pastoral and sacramental service to their parishioners, though in a traditional manner. In this respect, the compromise of allowing Latin as the language of the service may have enabled them to cloak religious changes in a familiar medium. For members of the uxorious hereditary clergy of the pre-Reformation Gaelic church, adherence to the Church of Ireland offered legitimacy for their wives and children, and even in anglicised inner Pale centres in Dublin and east Meath, conformity to Protestantism on the part of many parish clergy was seen as only skin-deep. Unsympathetic observers who came to Ireland from England gave a negative verdict on the post-1560 generation of the clergymen of the Church of Ireland. The residual clergy, comprising for the most part those who were ordained before 1558, were regarded as 'so void of knowledge of God and his will, that they know not his commandments' (Ronan 1930, 261). In almost half of the parishes of Meath, one of the wealthier Irish dioceses, Sir Henry Sidney reported to Queen Elizabeth I that the incumbents were 'Irish rogues, having very little Latin, less learning and civility' who lived on 'the gain of masses, dirges, shrivings and such like trumpery, godly abolished by your majesty' (Shirley 1851, 14-19).

By the 1590s there was emerging among Protestant leaders in Ireland a strong movement for the creation of a new ministry in the Church of Ireland. It was prompted in part by the chronic manpower crisis caused by the dying off or defection to the Catholic church of the old-style ministers, and was given momentum by the foundation of Trinity College in 1592. Already such a programme was beginning to bear fruit in the shape of the appointments of English graduate clergy to the chapter of St Patrick's cathedral, Dublin, under Archbishop Loftus's patronage. Less successful was the attempt to recruit Irish-speaking clergymen to be trained in the English universities for the ministry in the Gaelic western dioceses. While some graduates of Gaelic background were produced by the turn of the century, the level of their commitment to the state church was ultimately questionable. Overall, the standard of native ordinands remained low in the period before Trinity College began to produce its first graduates. Normally recourse was had to the appointment of lectors or reading ministers, instead of preaching ministers. Given the shortage of potential recruits in Ireland, it was to England that the Protestant leaders in Ireland in the early seventeenth century looked for the nucleus of a new ministry for the Anglican church.

By the opening decades of the new century, there was in being a small but increasing Protestant community in Ireland, though very much a minority of the island's population. Based largely in the city of Dublin and some other towns, it also encompassed newcomers in the planted regions of Munster, the midlands and later Ulster, where large numbers of Presbyterians settled. Hopes on the part of reformers for substantial numbers of converts to Protestantism in urban communities such as Kilkenny, Waterford, Cork, Limerick and Galway faded as the Counter-Reformation made significant progress among the civic communities. In the earlier seventeenth century, the character of the Reformation in Ireland was set. The small group of confirmed believers, whether of English or Irish background, was to be consolidated, no serious evangelisation of non-subscribers and non-English speakers being attempted. A distinctively Irish Protestant identity was forged through the Calvinistic tone of the Irish Articles of Faith of 1615 and the invocation by James Ussher, archbishop of Armagh, for example, of the continuity of the Anglican Church of Ireland from the early Irish church. For the state government, the extension of English rule throughout the newly-pacified island incorporated the promotion of the structures of the established church, though little attention was given to re-endowment or recovery of alienated resources. Until the 1640s, the unresolved question of toleration of the Catholic community was a constant distraction from the work of evolving a coherent Protestant confessional state. It was only after the convulsions of the mid-century period that a confident politico-ecclesiastical entity emerged, and that the full integration of the Reformation with the programme of state-building became feasible.

Bibliography

Bottigheimer, Karl S., 'The failure of the Reformation in Ireland: *une question bien posée*' in *Journal of Ecclesiastical History*, xxxvi (1985), pp. 196-207.

Bradshaw, Brendan, 'The opposition to the ecclesiastical legislation in the Irish Reformation parliament' in *Irish Historical Studies*, xvi (1968-9), pp. 285-303

— 'The Edwardian Reformation in Ireland, 1547-53' in *Archivium Hibernicum*, xxxiv (1976), pp. 83-99

Canny, Nicholas, 'Why the Reformation failed in Ireland: *une question mal posée*' in *Journal of Ecclesiastical History*, xxx (1979), pp. 423-50

Clarke, Aidan, 'Varieties of uniformity: the first century of the Church of Ireland' in W. J. Sheils and Diana Wood (eds.), *The churches, Ireland and the Irish: studies in church history*, xxv (York, 1989), pp. 105-19

Duffy, Eamon, *The stripping of the altars: traditional religion in England*, Yale University Press, New Haven, 1992

Ford, Alan, 'The Protestant Reformation in Ireland' in Ciaran Brady and Raymond Gillespie (eds.), *Natives and newcomers: essays on the making of Irish colonial society, 1534-1641*, Four Courts Press, Dublin, 1986

— McGuire, James and Milne, Kenneth (eds.), *As by law established: the Church of Ireland since the Reformation*, Four Courts Press, Dublin, 1995

— *The Protestant Reformation in Ireland, 1590-1641*, Four Courts Press, Dublin, 1997

— 'The Church of Ireland 1558-1634: a puritan church?' in Ford, Alan, McGuire, James and Milne, Kenneth (eds.), *As by law established: the Church of Ireland since the Reformation*, Four Courts Press, Dublin, 1995, pp. 52-68

Heal, Felicity, *Reformation in Britain and Ireland*, Clarendon Press, Oxford, 2003

Jefferies, H. A., *Priests and prelates of Armagh in the age of reformations, 1518-1558*, Four Courts Press, Dublin, 1997

— 'The early Tudor Reformation in the Irish Pale' in *Journal of Ecclesiastical History*, lii (2001), pp. 34-62

— 'The Irish parliament of 1560: the Anglican reforms authorised' in *Irish Historical Studies*, xxvi (1988), pp. 128-41.

Lennon, Colm, *Sixteenth century Ireland: the incomplete conquest*, Gill and Macmillan, Dublin, 1994

— 'The shaping of a lay community in the Church of Ireland, 1558-1640' in Gillespie, Raymond and Neely, W. G. (eds.), *The laity and the Church of Ireland, 1000-2000: all sorts and conditions*, Four Courts Press, Dublin, 2002, pp. 49-69

Meigs, Samantha, *The Reformations in Ireland: tradition and confessionalism, 1400-1690*, Gill and Macmillan, Dublin, 1997

Murray, James, 'Ecclesiastical justice and the enforcement of the Reformation: the case of Archbishop Browne and the clergy of Dublin' in Alan Ford, James McGuire and Kenneth Milne (eds.), *As by law established: the Church of Ireland since the Reformation*, Four Courts Press, Dublin, 1995, pp. 33-51

— 'The diocese of Dublin in the sixteenth century' in James Kelly and Dáire Keogh (eds.), *History of the diocese of Dublin*, Four Courts Press, Dublin, 2000, pp. 92-111

Ronan, Myles V., *The Reformation in Ireland under Elizabeth, 1558-1580*, Longmans Green and Company, London, 1930

Shirley, E. P. (ed.), *Original letters and papers in illustration of the history of the Church of Ireland during the reigns of Edward VI, Mary and Elizabeth*, London, 1851

This chapter replaces the lecture originally delivered by James Murray on 26 February 2002.

Recusancy and Counter-Reformation

Colm Lennon

An episode that took place in 1538 about two hundred yards from Christ Church Cathedral betokened the beginning of recusancy in the city of Dublin. At Sunday Mass, the parish priest of St Audoen's church off High Street, Fr James Humphrey, refused to read a new set of prayers referring to King Henry VIII as head of the church. As his curate started to do so instead, Father Humphrey bade the choir to strike up, drowning out the words of the prayers. Some parishioners reported Humphrey to the authorities, who promptly apprehended him for a breach of the Reformation statutes. He was soon released, however, resuming his priestly and administrative duties in St Audoen's and St Patrick's Cathedral (Lennon 1994, 113-14).

The Humphrey incident, albeit a minor one, may nonetheless be emblematic in the examination of the rise of recusancy and the Counter-Reformation in Ireland in the sixteenth and seventeenth centuries. It involved a priestly member of the affluent mercantile elite of Dublin, a group that was to be crucial in the state church's failure to win over the majority of the inhabitants of Ireland to Anglicanism. His recalcitrance, although not doctrinally-inspired, indicated discomfiture with the reforms in religion, and it was evidently shared by many (though not all) members of his congregation. The events moreover relate to the heart of the old walled town of Dublin, right under the gaze of the ecclesiastical and secular officials in St Patrick's and Dublin castle. And the leniency of Humphrey's treatment sprang both from the authorities' reluctance to make religious dissent a major issue at that time in Ireland, and also from divided counsels among the religious reformers as to how to cope with recusancy.

This chapter examines firstly how initial uneasiness about royal supremacy waxed into dissent over the doctrinal orthodoxy of the Church of Ireland among the generation that succeeded Humphrey's. Among the civic patricians in Dublin and elsewhere this commonly took the form of church papistry or nicodemism – public conformity to the liturgy masking private practice of Catholicism – in circumstances of minimal enforcement of the Reformation statutes. In order to understand secondly how this tentative recusancy among the urban and other elites was galvanised into a more active and open form of religious practice, we may refer to a series of traumatic occurrences in the mid-Elizabethan years. As a result, long-established institutions and residual resources were used to favour an alternative ecclesiastical system to that of the state church. It was upon these foundations that the agents of Catholic reform built in the seventeenth century to fashion a church in consonance with the decrees and ideals of the Council of Trent. In doing so they challenged not just the structures of the Church of Ireland but also the mores and attitudes of the members of the Catholic community in neighbourhoods such as St Audoen's parish. In examining finally how the reforms of the Catholic renewal impacted on the people of the parishes, I wish to raise very briefly the issue of the official toleration of Roman Catholicism within the state, a vital ideal of the missionary brand of Counter-Reformation.

The Irish Reformation parliament of 1560 legislated for a moderately Protestant Church of Ireland to be the official state church to which all must subscribe. The existing stock of church buildings was taken over by the Anglican establishment. Comparatively little attempt was made by church and state officials, however, to enforce conformity either to Queen Elizabeth's supremacy or to the liturgical reforms of Anglicanism. In this atmosphere of leniency in the 1560s and the 1570s, adherence to the old religious forms of worship was not uprooted, as officials followed the Queen's lead in not wishing to make windows into men's souls. Of course, considerable dislocation of the Catholic church organisation occurred, especially in areas of strong government jurisdiction such as Dublin, but continuity rather than change marked this earlier Elizabethan period. The unreconstructed beneficed clergy of the diocese, including those of the chapters of the two cathedrals, were criticised by the Protestant archbishop of Dublin, Adam Loftus, for dressing up old liturgical practices in vestments of the new order (Murray 2000, 108-19). According to the chief governor in 1562, lay leaders of the community were regarded as not taking the Reformation seriously, coming as they did to divine service 'as to a May game', being 'without discipline and utterly void of religion' (Ronan 1930, 69). Clearly, a full-scale campaign of evangelisation and educational reform, such as ultimately succeeded in England, was needed in Ireland to bring about conformity to the established church.

The nub of the problem for the English government in Ireland was a chronic lack of resources for the foundation of schools and colleges, and for attracting the most talented clergy to posts in the Irish church. Also key lay leaders in city and county, whose role as social and cultural exemplars was crucial in that highly-stratified and paternalistic society, were not offered incentives to acquiesce in the religious changes. Whereas the English gentry and merchant classes were granted lands and property of the dissolved chantries and religious fraternities to encourage compliance, the government in Ireland failed to suppress these institutions. Thus, while leading members of the community publicly subscribed to Anglicanism, there are clear signs of their private leanings towards Catholicism. Dublin officials such as James Bathe, John Plunket and James Stanihurst are notable among this coterie of 'church papists' who publicly attended divine service in the 1560s and 1570s but who heard mass privately in their dwellings. There they retained chaplains who were Catholic priests and tutors to their children. Some of the lay elites may have believed at that juncture that their dilemma could be solved by support for a moderate Christian humanist form of renewal that might eventually obviate confessional differences. Thus, for example, there was strong backing for an ultimately unsuccessful university project in 1570 that attracted the famous English scholar, Edmund Campion, to Dublin as potential rector. Its failure coincided with a hardening of confessional positions in Ireland as elsewhere, and the disappearance of the option of ambiguity.

While the public sacred places may have been taken over by the state church, much of the infrastructure of pre-Reformation religion remained intact. Besides their private chapels and chaplains, the lay leaders of the community controlled considerable resources of wealth and patronage within the ecclesiastical sphere. They had been granted extensive lands and property in the dissolution of the monasteries, and these possessions continued to yield tithe income from appropriated parishes and, in many cases, the right of advowson or appointment of clergy. Lay people had also founded and run chantries and confraternities in the late middle ages, appointing priests who were supernumerary to the diocesan system. One of the largest of all the confraternities was in St Audoen's parish, that dedicated to St Anne. With six altars in a purpose-built aisle, the confraternity became a powerful institution that continued on during the Reformation period. Possessed of large holdings of land from which it derived a sizeable income for chaplains' stipends, St Anne's numbered among its members some of the most influential men and women of the Dublin merchant community. The religious services at the heart of its liturgical round were probably curtailed with the more rigorous application of the act of uniformity from the 1570s and 1580s onwards, but the guild continued to play an important part in Dublin civic life: it functioned as a property-owning corporation, and a focus for sociability and commensality among the leading families (Lennon 1990, 6-25).

Events both at national and local levels in the mid-Elizabethan years proved to be decisive in the change from a passive to an active form of religious identification. The success of the imprisoned Archbishop Richard Creagh of Armagh in dissuading Catholic citizens from attendance at state church services caused him to be sent in 1575 from Dublin Castle to the Tower of London where he died of poisoning about twelve years later. Major revolts in support of the restoration of Roman Catholicism broke out in Leinster and Munster about 1580, and in the ensuing crackdown a number of clerical and lay leaders were executed as traitors. These included Archbishop Dermot O'Hurley of Cashel whose hanging at Hoggen Green in 1584 gave rise to a cult of his martyrdom among the pious citizens of Dublin. Another victim of the round-up of rebel sympathisers was Margaret Ball, a wealthy widow, who lived in the Merchant's Quay area. She had long maintained a chaplain and a school for Catholic pupils in her house. On the orders of her son, Walter, a Protestant, mayor of the city and an ecclesiastical commissioner, she was arrested for breaches of the statute of uniformity and detained in prison where she eventually died. The shock of the arrests, interrogations and executions of leading clerical and lay figures galvanised many in the rest of the community into determined action. Catholic recusancy came to constitute more than a mere refusal to conform to the state church but widened to embrace a more zealous activism. Encouraged by the work of martyrologists who celebrated the holy lives and deaths of the dead ones, the Catholic community assumed an identity apart as a separate confessional group.

This new assured stance from the 1580s and 1590s onwards encompassed the sending of offspring abroad to seminaries and university centres in Catholic Europe, some of which developed Irish colleges specifically for the training of Irish youths in the norms of the Council of Trent. Already in the south and west of the country, continentally-educated priests had begun to set up schools to catechise in the Tridentine mode. While Catholics may have had to abandon the churches, from the turn of the century they forged a distinctive network of places of worship, based in the homes of the gentry and merchant elites. Mass-houses sprang up in private residences in town and countryside where the returning seminary-trained priests found refuge as well as places to administer the sacraments. Increasingly, it

would appear, the resources that the Catholic recusants controlled were diverted towards the support of the Tridentine clergy,
and away from the maintenance of the fabric and personnel of
the state church. In effect an alternative church system came into
being in the early seventeenth century, paralleling the Anglican
one and moulding itself to the contours of recusant society. It
was funded by the income from ecclesiastical sources such as
tithes and religious fraternities that had remained in lay ownership, and was staffed by personnel appointed by virtue of
patronage rights inherited from the old system. Thus, even before a resident Counter-Reformation episcopacy had been established in many areas, a confident lay leadership had set up a
domesticated system of Catholic worship in concert with ardent
clergy returning from the continent.

In the parish of St Audoen's, the majority of families remained Catholic, as Archbishop Bulkeley confirmed in 1630:
'There are but sixteen Protestant houses in the parish, all the
rest, being above three parts, are recusants' ('Archbishop
Bulkeley's visitation of Dublin, 1630', p. 59). There was a natural
reluctance on the part of the older established families to abandon to the established church personnel (many of whom were
newcomers) the church with its chapels and tombs that had
been built by their ancestors in previous generations. The
Catholic parishioners appear to have baulked at contributing to
the maintenance of the parish clergy and the upkeep of the
buildings when the old services had been abrogated.
Archbishop Bulkeley complained that 'St Anne's guild hath
swallowed up all the church means which should be for the
minister and the reparation of the church' ('Archbishop
Bulkeley's visitation of Dublin, 1630', p. 59). Instead the recusant
majority directed the funds available from tithes and St Anne's
rents towards an alternative system of worship. A papal bull of
1569 that was later found in the muniments of St Anne's guild
directed that fraternity and chantry lands and properties should
be rented out only to Catholics, and the income expended on
priests' stipends. In the early seventeenth century it was reported

that the hall of the college of St Audoen's was a place of resort for mass-goers, and mass-houses were also operating in the parish in Mr Plunket's residence in Bridge Street and Nicholas Queytrot's in High Street. A Catholic priest, Fr Luke Rochford, was maintained by the Catholic families in the area among whom he administered the sacraments and educated the young.

Upon this informal system of nodal points of worship in city streets and rural manors the returning Counter-Reformation episcopate placed its own organisational stamp. The bishops and priests who spearheaded the Catholic renewal in the seventeenth century returned from the continental seminaries imbued with enthusiasm and zeal for the reforms of the Council of Trent. Indeed many of the Catholic agents were members of new orders such as the Society of Jesus and the Capuchins that had been founded specifically to foster devotion and practical charity. The emphasis in the work of these missioners was on reviving the sacramental life of the community, and instructing their hearers in the truths of the Catholic faith. In Ireland, however, where Catholicism was officially outlawed and the conditions for erecting this edifice of reform were far from propitious, it was with great difficulty that a resident episcopate was established to oversee the Irish Counter-Reformation. The ideal propounded by Trent was for resident bishops to implement the necessary changes within diocesan units that were to be under his close supervision and subject to his regular visitation. The focus of change at local level was to be the parish church, staffed by a seminary-trained priest who would administer the sacraments, preach the Tridentine norms and instil the piety of the Catholic renewal. But in Ireland, where, although the majority of the population came to adhere to Rome, the state was ruled by a Protestant regime, a different kind of church was to take shape, one that in effect shadowed the Anglican institution.

The Roman Catholic agents of reform succeeded in the early decades of the seventeenth century in setting up a church structure that was strong enough to withstand the extreme pressures of the 1640s and 1650s. Most Irish dioceses had resident bishops or vicars-general by the 1630s, and large numbers of regular and secular priests, many of them seminary-trained, were at work among the community. Diocesan and metropolitan synods were convened regularly to promulgate the decrees of the Council of Trent, making provision for the special circumstances obtaining in Ireland. Of particular concern to the Counter-Reformation bishops was the extirpation of excesses connected with Irish funerals, as well as the regularising of baptism and marriage practices. Strategically adapting the message of Trent to their flocks and congregations, the Catholic agents of renewal made use in their catechesis in Gaelic-speaking districts of Irish language texts that were being prepared on the continent at places such as Louvain, and in some cases printed there for wider distribution. The key to the success of the Catholic renewal in most areas indeed was this presentation of reform in the native idiom, though the Tridentine priests met some resistance to their imposition of new social mores that cut across traditional ways, in respect of pilgrimages to holy wells and burials, for example. Also unedifying turf wars took place between secular clergy and regulars over rights to preside at funerals.

During the years of rebellion in the 1640s and of the Cromwellian regime of the 1650s, most of this emergent church with its internal tensions was swept away. Bishops were banished, and the ministry of priests carried out with great difficulty. Yet, on the restoration of the monarchy in 1660, the process of rebuilding the shattered parish system began, and within two or three decades there was in being a functioning Catholic church again. In general, peaceful conditions were conducive to the nurturing of improved religious practice, but the changed political and social framework impinged upon the security of the pattern of priestly ministry centred on the private house. With the reduction in standing of the lay protectors of the Counter-Reformation system of worship – the county aristocrats and gentry, and the civic patricians – the Catholic community became more vulnerable to the whim of the state authorities. By and large, a *modus vivendi* had operated whereby the government officials had allowed the unofficial church to function, provided that due circumspection was observed in the matter of, for example, registration of births and marriages. What saved the Roman Catholic religion from coming under intolerable pressure after the restoration was the consideration of the consolidated Protestant interest in Ireland after 1660 that mass conversion of papists was economically undesirable and that an acceptable level of toleration was politic.

It may be useful to crystallise some of these developments in the local experience. In the parish of St Audoen the seeds of division were sown at the time of the Protestant and Catholic Reformations. The community was split along confessional lines, and even within families such as those of Ball and Ussher differences occurred over theological issues. There is no doubt that the Catholic community was inspirited by the ministry of the Counter-Reformation clergy. Out of the divergence there emerged two separate parish organisations, a Protestant one centred on the parochial church, and a Catholic one operating in mass-houses and chapels in the neighbourhood and eventually in a designated building on High Street. The fraternity of St Anne became synonymous with Catholic resistance to religious change and a long series of legal battles ensued between fraternity and parish officers over funds and the rights to property. Various compromises were worked out over the questions of the prebendary's salary and the responsibility of the fraternity towards the upkeep and repair of St Audoen's. Attempts to suppress or curtail the activities of the fraternity of St Anne continued right through the seventeenth century. These included subsuming those formerly known as chaplains within the new vicars choral of Christ Church Cathedral to boost its musical resources. The arrangements were not proceeded with, and the fraternity managed to reconstitute itself in 1653 under the cover of disarray within the established church caused by the Cromwellian settlement. After 1660 the life of the parish resumed its normal pattern.

It should be said that, denominational differences and litiga-

tion notwithstanding, there was little sign of sectarianism within
the parish. One gets the impression that the identity of the urban
Catholic community owed more to the older recusancy rather
than to the militancy of the Counter-Reformation. St Anne's fraternity remained essentially a civic institution, and quite different from the new-style sodality of the Catholic renewal, with its
tight clerical supervision. The fraternity may have had much in
common with the newly-developing Anglican system of
parochial charity. In a tightly-knit community the residual ties
of kinship and profession could override confessional differences. There is evidence that burials of Catholics continued in
the St Anne's chapel part of the St Audoen's complex down to
the 1630s. Personal relations remained good, despite the ritual-
ised skirmishing. In 1678, for example, when Mr Lucas Forrestal,
a merchant of Cook Street, was removed as a churchwarden because of his Catholicism, he 'freely offered one new large church
bible in folio and a common prayer book' (McCready 1886, 248).

Such interaction between the confessional groups in the loc-
alities was a characteristic of all but the most turbulent political
times in the seventeenth century. At critical moments the issue
of toleration of Catholicism flared into controversy, and the deli-
cate *modus vivendi* of local communities was threatened. In this
sense the politico-religious aspect of the Counter-Reformation
did have a huge bearing on the lives of ordinary Catholics, and
this aspect is addressed by way of conclusion.

Notwithstanding the success of the Counter-Reformation in
establishing a network of Catholic activities at local level, the
question of the toleration of the confessional position of the
Roman church was always problematic. The very survival of the
Counter-Reformation rested on the complaisance of the state
regime in its bishops and priests working on the ground, and indeed on the acceptance by the government of the whole concept
of a national episcopal framework supported by the Vatican.
Since the excommunication of the English monarch by the papacy
in 1570 the issue of the political loyalty of the Catholic subjects in
Ireland (and England) presented a crux. On the one hand, for

most of the following century or so the view of those Catholics prevailed who held that, although the monarch might be a heretic, he or she could nevertheless rule validly as long as freedom of conscience and worship was extended to the non-Anglican subjects. Antagonistic to this stance were those, including many clergy and laity of Gaelic background, who believed that a heretical monarch had forfeited the right to rule Ireland and should be replaced by a Catholic sovereign. For the most part, the protagonists of the former school were in the ascendant within the Roman church in the seventeenth century with the strong support of those of Old English descent, particularly the townspeople of Dublin and the other boroughs.

The nearest approach to a full restoration of the Catholic church within the state before the late seventeenth century came in the 1640s during the era of the confederation of Kilkenny. Then the Catholic confederates with the enthusiastic backing of the church authorities seemed close to agreeing full toleration with the representative of King Charles I, the marquis of Ormond. This would have raised the status of the Catholic community from that of an institution accorded mere arbitrary toleration at the whim of the monarch. The failure of this project was a major setback, and in the succeeding years feelings of distrust were compounded by the bitterness inspired by propagandist writings on both sides. After the restoration of the monarchy in 1660 uneasy toleration of Catholicism was resumed under the monarchy of Charles's son, but the work of organisation on the Catholic side had to be begun almost from scratch due to the dislocation of the 1650s. The fate of Archbishop Oliver Plunkett of Armagh, who was executed in 1681 for his alleged involvement in the Popish Plot, demonstrated the fragility of the position.

For a few years under King James II, a Catholic, his Irish co-religionists seemed to be on the verge of recapturing the initiative that was theirs very briefly at the end of the 1640s. The hope was that something more than mere prerogative toleration would be assured under James whose complaisance was taken for granted. One of the most symbolic events was the celebration of High Mass at Christ Church cathedral in 1689. Short of establishing a complete Catholic restoration, the Irish Catholic leadership asserted a position of religious equality with the Protestants under the rule of the Stuart monarchy. The Old English element among the Catholic population was set to be restored to the political nation on terms that they considered acceptable. But the Williamite victory and its aftermath cast doubt over all these aspirations, and the terms of the treaty of Limerick signed in 1691 were ominously vague and ambiguous. This promised Catholics such freedom of worship as was consistent with the laws of Ireland and such as they had enjoyed under Charles II. In the event the treaty was abrogated by a series of laws which underscored the exclusion of Catholics from political life, being accompanied by the final, fateful transfer of remaining Catholic property to Protestants. The era of the penal laws was born.

This assessment of recusancy and the Counter-Reformation has provided an opportunity to survey a phase in the history of Irish Christianity, specifically the formation of an Irish Catholic community in the early modern period. At first glance there appears to be a seamless transition from recusancy, that is, a refusal to countenance Protestantism, to full commitment to the Catholic renewal of the Counter-Reformation. A broadened understanding of the complexity of Irish society in that era, however, reveals that the process was more complicated. If by Counter-Reformation we mean the politico-religious movement that gave rise to a brand of Catholic nationalism, then the parts of this paper do not fit together very well. If, on the other hand, we stress the side of the Catholic renewal that promoted civic humanistic reform of institutions and mores, then there is a continuity from the world of the Elizabethan patricians to that of the Counter-Reformation agents. For the former group, their religious allegiance was part of their civic heritage, which they viewed themselves as having a duty to communicate to the wider island. Not all aspects of the clericalism of the Roman Counter-Reformation were compatible with this recusant cultural milieu, any more than were the innovations of the state reformers. As long as their political and religious loyalties were not brought into open conflict, these erstwhile recusants could retain their wonted place in society, but once a painful choice had to be made between them, the essential vulnerability of their position was revealed.

Bibliography

'Archbishop Bulkeley's visitation of Dublin, 1630', ed. Myles V. Ronan, in *Archivium Hibernicum* viii (1941), pp. 56-98

Bottigheimer, Karl S., 'The failure of the Reformation in Ireland: *une question bien posée*' in *Journal of Ecclesiastical History* xxxvi (1985), pp. 196-207.

Bradshaw, Brendan, 'The Reformation in the cities: Cork, Limerick and Galway, 1534-1603' in John Bradley (ed.), *Settlement and Society in Medieval Ireland: Studies presented to Francis Xavier Martin, O.S.A*, Boethius Press, Kilkenny 1988, pp. 445-76

— 'English Reformation and identity formation in England and Wales' in Brendan Bradshaw and Peter Roberts, ed., *British Consciousness and Identity: The Making of Britain, 1533-1707*, Cambridge University Press, Cambridge 1998, pp. 43-111

Corish, P. J., *The Catholic Community in the Seventeenth and Eighteenth Centuries*, Helicon, Dublin,1981

Cunningham, Bernadette, 'The culture and ideology of Irish Franciscan historians at Louvain, 1607-1650' in Ciaran Brady, ed., *Ideology and the Historians*, Lilliput Press, Dublin 1991

Forrestal, Alison, *Catholic Synods in Ireland, 1600-1690*, Four Courts Press, Dublin 1998

Lennon, Colm, *The Lords of Dublin in the Age of Reformation*, Irish Academic Press, Dublin 1989

— 'The chantries in the Irish Reformation: the case of St Anne's guild, Dublin, 1550-1630' in R. V. Comerford, Mary Cullen, J. R. Hill and Colm Lennon, ed., *Religion, Conflict and Coexistence in Ireland: Essays in Honour of Monsignor Patrick J. Corish*, Gill and Macmillan, Dublin 1990, pp. 6-25

— *Sixteenth Century Ireland: The Incomplete Conquest*, Gill and Macmillan, Dublin 1994

— *An Irish Prisoner of Conscience of the Tudor Era: Archbishop Richard Creagh of Armagh, 1523-86*, Four Courts Press, Dublin 2000

— 'Mass in the manor house: the Counter-Reformation in Dublin, 1560-1630' in James Kelly and Dáire Keogh, ed., *History of the Diocese of Dublin*, Four Courts Press, Dublin 2000, pp. 112-26

— 'Religious wars in Ireland: plantations and martyrs of the Catholic church' in Brendan Bradshaw and Dáire Keogh, ed., *Christianity in Ireland: Revisiting the Story*, Columba Press, Dublin 2002, pp. 86-95

— 'The shaping of a lay community in the Church of Ireland, 1558-1640' in Raymond Gillespie and W. G. Neely (ed.), *The Laity and the Church of Ireland, 1000-2000: All Sorts and Conditions*, Four Courts Press, Dublin 2002, pp. 49-69

McCready, C. T., 'History of St Audoen's Church, Dublin', *Irish Builder* 27 (1 Sept. 1868)

Meigs, Samantha, *The Reformations in Ireland: Tradition and Confessionalism, 1400-1690*, Gill and Macmillan, Dublin 1997

Murray, James. 'The diocese of Dublin in the sixteenth century' in James Kelly and Dáire Keogh, ed., *History of the Diocese of Dublin*, Four Courts Press, Dublin 2000, pp. 92-111

Ó hAnnracháin, Tadhg, *Catholic Reformation in Ireland: The mission of Rinuccini, 1645-1649*, Oxford University Press, Oxford 2002

Ó Siochrú, Micheál, *Confederate Ireland, 1642-1649: A Constitutional and Political Analysis*, Four Courts Press, Dublin 1999

Ronan, Myles V., *The Reformation in Ireland under Elizabeth, 1558-1580*, Longmans Green and Company, London, 1930

Delivered 7 May 2002

The Ascendancy and the Penal Laws

James Kelly

Given the centrality of religious allegiance in the struggle for political and ideological pre-eminence in post-Reformation Ireland, and the near universal acceptance by ruling elites of the legitimacy of repression as a means of eliding dissent, one of the more striking features of the code of anti-Catholic legislation known as the Penal Laws[1] is its late generation. This is not to suggest that there was no domestically generated anti-Catholic regulation prior to the 1690s when what is denominated the 'penal era' may be said to have commenced. But, since the authority of Protestantism in Ireland was sharply contested until that point, and the engagement of the British Crown, which constituted the ultimate authority in the kingdom of Ireland, was fitful and inconsistent, circumstances were not conducive to the inauguration at an earlier date of a systematic body of anti-Catholic regulation. Saliently, this contrasted with the situation in England where a substantial body of law aimed at inhibiting Catholic worship and protecting the state by, among other regulations, disarming Catholics was already in existence.[2] Ireland's Protestants were no less convinced of the advisability of a similar regime to safeguard and to protect them against the hostile intentions of Irish Catholics, but it was not until their dominance was assured by the decisive triumph of the Williamites over the Jacobites in 1689-91 that they were in a position to make that aspiration a reality. Impelled at the outset by the fervent conviction (borne out of harsh experience) that their continued ascendancy, politically as well as religiously, demanded that they take all necessary measures to safeguard their position, they were enabled over a period of two decades to implement a

sequence of ambitious laws that dramatically attenuated the lib-
erties of Catholics politically, religiously and economically.
Further, more specific, restrictions ensued during the early
Hanoverian era, for though one can identify a palpable easing in
the belief in Britain and Ireland in the efficacy of repression as a
means of enfeebling Catholicism from the 1720s, the conviction
that the Penal Laws were crucial to the well being of Irish
Protestants remained strong. It was not sufficient to pre-empt a
slowly appreciating acceptance within the ranks of liberal
Protestantism of the argument that Catholics should be allowed
practice their religion and earn a livelihood free of restriction,
which contributed to the repeal of the Penal Laws that addressed
these concerns between 1778 and 1792. Opposition to the removal
of the restrictions on the admission of Catholics to the political
process proved more enduring, for though the right to vote was
restored in 1793, the subsequent invigoration of anti-Catholic
sentiment in Britain as well as Ireland in response to the challenge
of revolutionary radicalism ensured that resistance to the demand
of Catholics to the right to sit in parliament remained integral to
the politics of Irish Protestants until the late 1820s.

I

Though the economic and social foundations of what historians
term 'Protestant ascendancy' were already firmly in place[3] by
the time the armies commanded by William of Orange encountered James II's Jacobite forces at the Battle of the Boyne in July
1690, the triumph of the former in this encounter and of the
Williamite forces in the war of which it was a part, had a decisive
impact on the political landscape. Prior to the outbreak of hostilities Irish Protestants were confined, in the absence of parliament, which neither Charles II nor James II was disposed to con-
vene on a regular basis, to the proclamation as the primary
means of implementing their political and administrative decisions. This proved a useful device at times of crisis, but its intrinsic
ephemerality, allied to the fact that it originated with the Privy
Council, which was hardly representative of the Protestant in-

terest at large, meant it was not an entirely satisfactory mode of proceeding. This was underlined during James II's controversial reign when the Council became increasingly unresponsive to Protestant concerns. However, the events that impacted most deeply on Protestant consciousness were not the attempts made between 1685 and 1688 to empower Catholics at the expense of Protestants,[4] but the experience of war and exile they endured following James' deposition in November 1688, and the threat posed by the Jacobite parliament in 1689 that thousands of named Protestants would forfeit their lives as well as their properties if they did not publicly commit to support James II's claim to the throne. Moreover, the realisation, if the Jacobites prevailed, that Protestants could anticipate long-term social, economic and political marginalisation and unrelenting religious oppression deepened and extended the conviction, already widely embraced within the Protestant interest, of the urgency of not allowing Catholics any further opportunity to exercise power and influence. This is why so many Protestants deemed the terms of the Treaty of Limerick, which concluded hostilities in Ireland and which seemed to offer Irish Catholics the promise of religious toleration and, if still in arms, the prospect of retaining their real estate, so unendurable.

Meanwhile, such views were reinforced in the aftermath of the formal conclusion of hostilities in Ireland in the autumn of 1691 by the realisation that the defeat of James II in Ireland was only one aspect of the ongoing struggle upon which William of Orange was embarked with the most powerful Catholic county in Europe – France – and that failure in his larger task of curbing the relentless ambitions of Louis XIV could set the recent gains in Ireland at naught.[5] Moreover, continuing disquiet in Ireland, attributable to vestigial military and criminal elements that were variously labelled tories and rapparees, served to heighten unease and to give substance to proliferating rumours that the arrival of a French expeditionary force would stimulate a renewed outburst of Catholic insurrection. These concerns were fuelled further by the open avowal by Catholic clergy of support for

James II and for France, and their continued involvement in intrigues on behalf of both during the 1690s was indicative, not just of where their loyalties lay, but of their eagerness to promote the extension to Ireland of an absolutist-style monarchy along French lines. This was no less odious to Irish Protestants than it was to their English equivalents, and their unease on this score was augmented and reinforced by their perception that Catholicism and absolutism were at one in their attachment to a form of government that was intrinsically despotic.

In addition, Protestant antipathy towards Catholicism was informed by strong theological convictions borne out of the belief that Catholics pursued a corrupted version of the religion that God intended, that the bible sanctioned, and that there were legitimate grounds for deeming the pope the antichrist. All Protestants were not so categorical, but the belief borne out of religious conviction as well as by history that Catholics would, if they were given the opportunity, seek remorselessly to extirpate Protestants (as they had attempted in 1641), on the grounds that there could be no tolerance of heretics, gave added impetus to the more obvious political arguments in support of a policy justifying the implementation of a body of law that protected Protestants in Ireland against the all too likely prospect of a repetition of recent doleful events.

II

Though convinced of their necessity, Irish Protestants were ill placed to progress their objective of introducing laws to secure them against a Catholic revanche on the conclusion of the Williamite War. The expectation among ministers and officials, which was not contradicted by hazy memories of proceedings in the Irish parliament, which had last met in formal session in 1666, was that Irish MPs would accede to the subordinate legislative role defined for it according to the interpretation of Poynings' Law favoured by the Crown, and that the key decisions as to the nature and content of anti-Catholic legislation would be made at governmental level.[6] Thus in 1691, a year be-

fore the Irish parliament assembled, it was determined at
Westminster to replace the requirement that officeholders and
others previously enjoined to subscribe to the Oath of
Supremacy authorised in 1558 (1 Eliz. 1, chap 1) should subscribe
instead to new 'oaths of allegiance [to William III and Queen
Mary] and abhorrence [of James II]' and to a declaration deny-
ing transubstantiation, which effectively closed off parliament
and officerships of the courts to Catholics. This met with no objections from Irish Protestants, who welcomed the introduction
of such confessional barriers, but their elected representatives
were no less determined that their legislative function should
not be a passive one, and that their role should not be confined
to approving or rejecting measures prepared at the Irish Council
Board and previously ratified at the English Council in accordance with the restrictive official interpretation of Poynings' Law.
Determined to assert their entitlement as equal subjects of the
Crown to possess the same rights as Englishmen, they forced the
prorogation of the 1692 session by asserting their 'sole right' to
raise financial legislation. Obliged, as a result, to compromise to
accommodate Protestant aspirations, the 1695 session was a
turning point in the history of the Irish parliament as in return
for voting the necessary financial revenue to fund the administration of the kingdom, MPs were afforded a direct say in the
initiation of legislation.[7] Significantly, the measures they
favoured included two important Penal Laws: the first was a
prohibition on Catholics publicly operating schools and a ban
on Catholics going abroad to be educated (7 Will III, chap 4); the
second a provision for disarming Catholics that, *inter alia*, obliged them to surrender 'all' arms and ammunition in their posses-
sion, unless they came under the terms of the Treaty of Limerick
or were issued with a licence from the Privy Council, and to sell
'any horse, gelding or mare of £5 value' on receipt of an offer of
five guineas from a Protestant (7 Will III, chap 5). Since both
these measures could be justified on security grounds, they cannot simply be labelled anti-Catholic, but the fact that MPs also
chose during the same session to apply a Protestant definition of

those days that were appropriate for 'holy days' and to con-
demn those celebrated by Catholics 'dedicated to some saint, or
pretended saint' as an occasion of 'idleness, drunkenness and
vice' indicates that more than the interests of the state were at
issue (7 Will III, chap 14). It certainly made it clear that the
Protestant membership of the Irish parliament felt justified in
initiating and approving legislation targeted specifically at con-
fining Catholics.

Significantly, this set the pattern for what was to follow. Over
the course of the next seven years, requiring only two sessions of
parliament, the core elements of the Penal Laws directed at enfeebling Irish Catholics socially, politically, economically and religiously were admitted to the statute book. In pursuing this
course of action, Irish Protestants had the support of a majority
of English politicians, who were of one mind with them on the
advisability of restricting the opportunities and freedoms of
Catholics and Catholicism. Indeed, so long as a measure was not
inconsistent with the provisions of the Treaties of Limerick and
Galway, most anti-Catholic regulations emanating from Ireland
were virtually assured of a positive welcome at Whitehall. This
is not to say that there were not disagreements on points of detail, or that there were no occasions when ministerial readiness
to dilute a particular provision in response to the diplomatic lob-
bying of Catholic powers was not unwelcome in Ireland, but the
close co-operation manifest in 1703-04 in devising the key act to
prevent the further growth of popery is indicative that they
were in agreement on the strategy to be pursued in respect of
'the Catholic problem'.

It was this shared attitude that facilitated the ratification in
1697 of acts that sought to banish 'all papists exercising any
ecclesiastical jurisdiction and all regulars of the popish clergy' (9
Will III, chap. 21); to preclude 'Protestants intermarrying with
Papists' (9 Will III, chap 3); to prevent the return of subjects who
had gone to France (9 Will III, chap 5); to prohibit Catholics having access to fire arms by prescribing their employment as
'fowlers' to Protestants (10 Will III, chap 8); and to 'prevent

Papists being solicitors' (10 Will III, chap 13). This was a weighty series of additions to the extant corpus of anti-Catholic legislation, and the Catholic Church, particularly, was seriously weakened by the 'banishment' of hundreds of regular clergy and a majority of its episcopate.[8] However, this left the still numerous ranks of the secular clergy unregulated, and in 1703-04 a registration procedure was approved, which stipulated that only one secular Catholic priest would be authorised for each civil parish, and which directed that those who failed to register would be obliged to leave the country (2 Anne, chap 7). In addition, in order to curtail the surreptitious and unregulated movement of 'bishops, deans, fryers, jesuits and other regulars' from continental Europe 'under the disguise of being Popish secular priests', the penalties for infringing the prohibition on their entry into the country were strengthened (2 Anne, chap 3). Taken together with the deliberate refusal of the framers of the registration provisions for the secular clergy to provide for the replacement of old, retired or deceased clergy, the expectation was that the capacity of the Catholic Church to minister would atrophy over time and that this would pave the way for the dramatic growth of the Church of Ireland, which the efforts of the various Protestant societies for the reformation of manners active at this time also contrived to promote.[9]

In order to increase the attractiveness of this option to Catholics, but also to ensure that the economic resources of the country remained firmly within Protestant control, 1704 also saw the enactment of the deceptively innocuously titled 'Act to prevent the further growth of popery'. This, the most comprehensive of all the Penal Laws, provided, *inter alia*, for the sanctioning of Protestants who converted to Catholicism and for the raising of Catholic orphans as Protestants; it prohibited land passing from Protestant to Catholic ownership by purchase or inheritance; it restricted the capacity of Catholics to lease land to 31 years; it ordained that land in Catholic ownership should descend by gavelkind rather than primogeniture, except where an eldest son conformed, in which case his right to possess the undivided estate took precedence over that of his parents; and it stipulated that Catholics seeking to exercise the franchise must show evidence of having subscribed to the oaths of allegiance and abjuration (2 Anne, chapter 6).

With the ratification of this measure, the main provisions of the Penal Laws were in place. However, despite the best efforts of all involved, the regulations proved incomplete and deficient, and a host of additions and amendments were required in the course of the following decades. For example, in 1707 (6 Anne, chap 6), 1727 (1 Geo II, chap 20) and 1733 (7 Geo II, chap 5) explanatory acts were approved to the 1697 act to prevent Catholics practising as solicitors, while in 1727 restrictions comparable to those already in place to regulate solicitors were extended to practising barristers, who, among other demands, were required to subscribe to the oaths of allegiance and abjuration (1 Geo II, chap 20). Twelve years previously, in 1715, the 1703 requirement that Catholics seeking to exercise the franchise should provide proof of having subscribed to the oaths of allegiance and abjuration was tightened (it now had to be taken 6 months in advance and on the election day) (2 Geo I, chap 19), culminating in 1727 in the introduction of a formal prohibition on Catholics voting (1 Geo II, chap 9). Meanwhile, in 1705, further refinements were made to the 1697 and 1703 laws for 'banishing popish clergy' (4 Anne, chap 2), while in 1709 a substantial act for 'explaining' the 1704 'act to prevent the further growth of popery' was required to accommodate the plethora of errors, omissions and loopholes identified to date in this and others among the extant corpus of anti-Catholic regulations on the statute book. The most controversial aspect of this bill was the suggestion that 'all registered popish priests' should subscribe to the oath of abjuration before 25 March 1710, but this was of less material import than the inauguration of a statutory prohibition on Catholics in trade keeping more than two apprentices at a time (8 Anne chap 3).

The extension of the remit of the Penal Laws to embrace such ostensibly quotidian matters as apprenticeships reflected the parallel efforts of the corporations of Cork and Dublin, and presumably elsewhere, to ensure that local Protestants had a permanent competitive advantage over their Catholic competitors in trade and industry.[10] It is also a pointer to the fact that, as well as amending defective or deficient regulations, new and additional penal provisions continued to be introduced long after the passing of what is traditionally presented as the high point of the making of anti-Catholic legislation spanning the years 1691-1709. There was less obvious need for major anti-Catholic legislative initiatives once the Hanoverians were safely placed on the throne in 1714, but the Irish parliament continued to propose significant anti-Catholic legislation into the 1750s. Many of these interventions were, as previously observed of earlier laws, of the nature of refinements to extant regulations: for example, amendments were authorised in 1739 to the law on Catholics bearing arms (13 Geo II, chap 6); in 1745 and 1755 to the law barring Catholics from entering into foreign service (19 Geo II, chap 7; 29 Geo II, chap 5); and in 1727, 1735, 1745 and 1749 to the extant regulations dating from 1697 aimed at preventing marriage with Protestants (12 Geo I, chap 3; 9 Geo II, chap 11; 19 Geo II, chap 11; 23 Geo II, chap 10). However, the early Hanoverian era also witnessed the extension of the remit of the Penal Laws to engage with new or previously overlooked issues. For example, the prohibition on Catholics becoming high or petty constables dates from 1715 (2 Geo I, chap 10); on Catholic becoming watchmen from 1719 (6 Geo I, chap 10); on Catholics and converts from Catholicism with a 'popish' wife acting as justices of the peace from 1733 (7 Geo II, chap 6); and on Catholics serving on juries from 1735 (9 Geo II, chap 3). If it is clear from this that there are good grounds for broadening the chronological definition of the 'penal era' beyond the narrower parameters currently in vogue, it is also apparent, based on the range and compass of the laws themselves and on the temporal connection one can draw between their date of enactment and major invasion scares (1719, 1722-3, 1733-4, 1739 and 1745), when Protestant anxieties were invariably much heightened, that the enthusiasm for anti-

Catholic regulation had well passed by the latter date. This is consistent with Sean Connolly's argument that the Penal Laws must be seen as an *ad hoc* response on the part of the Protestant interest in Ireland to problems as they arose. This is not to say, however, that the provisions of the laws were *ad hoc*; while certain matters – land, religion and the legal profession – attracted and required greater legislative attention than others such as education, the combined corpus of the Penal Laws provided the Protestant elite in Ireland with a widely embracing code of laws whereby they could not only safeguard their ascendancy against challenge from within from the Catholic majority, but could also consign the Catholic population to a clearly subordinate position.

III

Much depended, of course, on the manner in which the Laws were applied and, while the absence of court records means this is difficult to establish with any confidence, the prevailing impression is that their strict enforcement was limited to those years – 1709, 1715, 1719, 1722, 1733-4, 1739 and 1745 – of greatest Protestant unease. There are good grounds to concur with this conclusion though it makes insufficient allowance for variation between laws and different categories of laws, and for a more general variation over time. Taking the latter point first; a sustainable case can be advanced that much of the extant corpus of anti-Catholic regulation was applied as thoroughly as the administrative capacity of the early modern state allowed during the 1690s and the first two decades of the eighteenth century. Thus, for example, the burgers of Cork ensured the Protestantism of their corporation by requiring from 1694 that all freemen should subscribe to the 1691 'oaths of allegiance and supremacy [sic]'.[12] The Society of Kings Inns did likewise by instructing in 1705 that nobody should be 'admitted to the bar and practice as a barrister' who had not taken the sacrament according to the rites of the Church of Ireland.[13] Catholic property owners too were compelled to go to extraordinary lengths to keep their estates together and to evade the more onerous provisions against landownership.[14] But the most vivid, and visible, arena of repression during this early phase was the religious sphere. There, following on the forced departure of hundreds of regular clergy and ecclesiastics in the late 1690s, those that remained lived their life in the shadow of imprisonment. This threat was at its greatest in the context of invasion scares such as occurred in 1708-10 and 1715 when churches and mass houses were closed down and orders given to magistrates and others to take into custody whatever clergy they could. Among those arrested were Bishop Patrick Donnelly of Dromore (1706) and Archbishop Edmund Byrne of Dublin (1718). The effect of such orders, given in 1708, 1714 and 1716, was not just to interrupt but also severely to disrupt the Catholic Church in Ireland. Catholics believed, indeed, that the object was 'to destroy the Catholic religion', which flatters the capacity of the Protestant state to achieve this end, and exaggerates the intensity and the impact of the repression to which Catholics were subject.[15] The experience of repression was acutely uncomfortable for those members of the Catholic clergy who came to the authorities' notice, but they were invariably short-lived and separated by what were, by comparison, long intervals during which the authorities were not disinclined to look sympathetically upon Catholic clerics and others, incarcerated for infringing the Penal Laws, who sought to have their penalties commuted.[16] The hope rather than the expectation of Protestants was that the distress and discomfort under which Catholics operated because of the Penal Laws, allied to their assumption that Protestantism was a naturally superior religion because it was more consistent with God's vision of a Christian religion, would encourage mass conversion. This was not the case, but the application of the laws, however fitful this may appear in retrospect, served effectively to inhibit the operations of the Catholic Church while the disempowerment of the Catholic laity, vividly illustrated by the fact that a paltry 134 Catholic males were licensed to bear arms in 1713, indicated that the laws also effectively secured Protestants against the prospect of a domestically inspired Catholic uprising that would alter the current disposition of political and economic power.[17]

Significantly, few Irish Protestants felt particularly secure in the first half of the eighteenth century. Preachers, like Rowland Davies, dean of Cork, and William Hamilton, archdeacon of Armagh, warned their co-religionists in published sermons to remain vigilant since, in the words of the former, 'while we have papists among us, we shall never want an enemy, nor an executioner fitted to our destruction'.[18] As a consequence, despite the smooth inauguration of the Hanoverian succession in 1714, Irish Protestants remained prone to bouts of acute anti-Catholic hysteria. This was at the root of the attempt, spearheaded by the Irish Commons, in 1723 to secure approval for 'an act for explaining and amending the acts to prevent the growth of popery' that proposed to make it treasonable, and therefore a capital offence, for a registered priest who had not subscribed to the oath of abjuration to say mass and for non-registered clergy even to be in the kingdom after 25 March 1724. Resistance at the Irish Privy Council to what was described famously by Archbishop William King as a 'barbarous' regulation ensured that the bill forwarded to the British Privy Council was shorn of its more egregious elements, but it is significant that it was transmitted from Ireland with the message that it was 'a necessary support of the Protestant interest in this kingdom'.[19]

Ministers disagreed and the bill did not become law, but of greater significance for the future of the policy of repressing Catholicism were the differences the measure highlighted within Irish Protestantism and between the political elites in Britain and Ireland as to the efficacy of this strategy. The modest number of converts to the Church of Ireland – though a satisfying proportion were from the landed elite – certainly encouraged such thinking, while the willingness of a small number of Catholic gentry to offer allegiance to George II on his accession in 1727 was also heartening. The diminution in state support for the prosecution of Catholic clergy (in County Limerick, for example, the 1726 assizes were the first in many years at which no unregistered priest was presented, while judges on circuit 'recommended moderation to the magistrates'[20]) was also indicative, while a number of notable voices, of whom the most eminent were Bishop Josiah Hort of Ferns and Archbishop Edward Synge of Tuam, were prepared openly to question the appositeness of current tactics on the grounds that coercion was illjudged when it was not simply counter-productive.[21]

Such sentiments were received with great scepticism by a majority of Irish Protestants for whom the reports, relayed in great detail and discussed with great animation, of the execution of Protestants at Thorn in the Catholic kingdom of Poland in 1725 proved vastly more compelling. Reflexively disposed to conclude from the vivid images of massacre, which the annual commemoration of the outbreak of the 1641 rebellion perpetuated among the Protestant community at large, that they would be subject to the same experience as their Polish co-religionists should the restrictions in force against Catholics in Ireland be relaxed, some Protestants talked openly of 'revenge'. This was not a realistic option, but the readiness of Protestants in the late 1720s and early 1730s to deem Catholics 'insolent', and to draw hostile notice to the 'great numbers of Popish Priests, particularly of Monks, Fryars and Jesuits' in the country prompted calls for the more strict execution of the existing Penal Laws and facilitated the admission of further specific restrictions onto the statute book.[22] Such sentiments were reinforced by the perception fostered by the 1731 report into the 'state of popery' that the Catholic church was stronger than it had been a decade earlier. This contributed to a surge in prosecutions and in general anti-Catholic activity in the early 1730s, peaking in 1734, and to support for an alternative, educational, strategy that took institutional form in the shape of the Charter Schools (1733), which had an avowedly proselytising agenda.

Though it was not admitted at the time, both the foundation of the Charter Schools and the specific character of such anti-Catholics laws as were admitted to the statute book during the

reign of George II demonstrated that the highpoint of the policy
of anti-Catholic repression had passed. It may not be said to
have concluded in any formal fashion until the mid-1740s when
the passivity of the Catholics of Ireland during the winter of
1745-46, as Charles Edward Stuart and his Jacobite cohorts
briefly threatened the stability of the Hanoverian state, was
commended by the then lord lieutenant, the Earl of Chesterfield.
This did not mean that Catholic clerics, particularly members of
the episcopate, who were discovered in the country illegally,
were immune from arrest and detention, that Catholic gentry
who were caught bearing arms escaped prosecution or that
other infractions were not penalised,[23] but the mid-century witnessed a palpable thaw in the hostility with which Catholics
were regarded within the ranks of the Protestant elite.

It was encouraged, moreover, by the more profound sea
change that took place in British opinion, which resulted in the
rejection at the British Privy Council in the 1730s and 1740s of a
variety of legislative measures emanating from the Irish parliament whose purpose was to tighten still further the bonds of repression against Catholics.[24] Though some British politicians,
such as Lord Chesterfield, were disposed to explain the attitude
of Irish Protestants simplistically by reference to the fact that
'they are in general still at the year 1689, and have not shook off
any religious or political prejudice that prevailed at that time',
Lord Chancellor Bowes was characteristically more accurate
when he confided to one of his English correspondents that it
was the perception of Irish Protestants 'that the safety and property of the kingdom [depends upon] those laws'.[25] Be that as it
may, the conclusion, reached by one well-informed official in
1750, 'that no law for the benefit of Protestantism and discour-
agement of Popery can be passed in England' was not without
import or effect on the actions of the Irish legislature, though it
had little obvious impact on the generality of Irish Protestants at
the time.[26] Indeed, so long as the Jacobite Court sustained its
claim to succeed to the British throne and was permitted by the
papacy to nominate to Irish Catholic bishoprics, Irish Protestants

felt entirely justified in their contention that the Penal Laws
were both justified and necessary. Their continuing perception
of Catholicism as a tyrannical confession that was committed to
the bloody extirpation of Protestant heresy, if necessary by the
auto da fé, reinforced them in this conviction.

IV

The death in 1766 of the 'Old Pretender' (James III) and the subsequent withdrawal from the Stuart Court of the right to nominate to Irish bishoprics, combined with the effusive declarations
of loyalty from the representatives of Irish Catholicism on the
accession, in 1760, of George III to the throne, helped dilute such
concerns. However, the vitriolic local response among the 'red
hot Protestants' of County Tipperary to a surge in agrarian dis-
content conducted by the Whiteboys, and the manipulation of
due process to secure the execution of Fr Nicholas Sheehy in
1766, was a strong pointer to the likelihood of strong resistance
among the Protestant population at large to any attempt to satisfy
Catholic wishes that the Penal Laws might be repealed.[27] Many
Irish Protestants were content by this date to accept that the laws
against the practice by Catholics of their religion need no longer
be enforced, but they were distinctly more attached to the restrictions on Catholics owning land, on opposing their right to
trade on the same terms as Protestants, and uncompromisingly
resistant to any attempt to interfere with the barriers on Catholic
participation in the political process.

Informed by the conviction (the prolix professions of loyalty
emanating from the Catholic Committee notwithstanding) 'that
the generality of [Catholics] are disaffected to the Government,
and wait only a favourable opportunity to cast it off', Irish
Protestants were acutely suspicious of such attempts as were
made in the 1760s and early 1770s to ease the burden of disabilities on Catholics.[28] Moreover, those who proffered a contrary
view were afforded scant respect; thus a call made in 1763 by an
'English Protestant resident in Ireland' for Catholic relief was
vigorously reprobated on the grounds that Catholics were

committed 'to destroy all civil and religious liberty'.[29] Bishop
Charles Agar of Cloyne was no less categorical a decade later
when the matter at issue was a 'popish mortgage bill': 'the intol-
erant principles of the popish religion and its enmity to the civil
rights of mankind' rendered it impossible, he protested, consistent with 'the future security of our constitution in Church and
State', to agree to any dilution of the Penal Laws.[30] Few were as
cogent and effective as Bishop Agar in articulating this position,
but his point of view was so well supported within the generality
of the Protestant interest that there seemed little likelihood of
the Irish parliament agreeing to repeal a significant strand of the
Penal Laws in the near future.

This was, and it would in all likelihood have remained the
case had the British government not felt obliged for its own reasons to intervene in the late 1770s. Compelled by the needs of
the British military machine, which required Catholic recruits,
the government calculated that this could best be assured by
agreeing to the repeal of the major disabilities limiting the entitlement of Catholics to lease and to purchase land. Irish
Protestants, including Henry Grattan who subsequently championed the cause of Catholic relief, were ill at ease, but only the
most diehard opposed its admission to the statute book, and it
became law in 1778.[31] Inspired by this, and by the prospect of
overcoming the debilitating sectarian divisions that stood in the
way of the concept of an inclusive 'nation', Grattan and his
Patriot colleagues successfully secured the repeal of a majority
of the non-political Penal Laws in 1782. It was a moment of great
symbolic as well as real significance, and it was widely anticipated among the leaders of the Catholic Committee, who had
dextrously led the Catholic interest, and of the Patriots in parliament that further relief would not be long delayed. However,
because the next major category of disability under which the
Catholics operated appertained to their exclusion from the political process, it was soon apparent that many Patriots, who enter-
tained few or no reservations with the concession to Catholics of
all rights consistent with the maintenance intact of a 'Protestant

constitution', were unwilling to agree further concessions. As a result, the attempts made in 1783-4 to secure the admission of Catholics to the franchise proved stillborn because of debilitating divisions within the ranks of the advocates of parliamentary reform from whence the demand came.[32] More crucially, for Catholics it took the issue of the Penal Laws off the political agenda for the remainder of the decade during which time the ideological arsenal of conservative Protestantism, which could be relied upon to express the atavistic unease of the Protestant interest at large with the principle of making concessions to Catholics, was greatly augmented by the elaboration of the rhetoric of 'Protestant ascendancy'. This was prompted in the first instance by clerical concern that the opposition of the Rightboys agrarian movement to the payment of tithes to the clergy of the Church of Ireland was an assault on the Established Church.[33] By the early 1790s, when the question of Catholic enfranchisement had moved centre stage once more, this rhetoric was taken up and applied with even greater ideological impact in support of resistance to any alteration to the 'Protestant constitution in church and state'. A vigorous rearguard resistance was orchestrated in support of the constitutional *status quo*, but once the British government had determined in 1792 that Catholics should be allowed to vote, the 'exclusive pre-eminence' that Irish Protestants had enjoyed in the Irish constitution was no more, and many Protestants forecast that it was only a matter of time until Catholics were admitted on full and equal terms with Protestants to the political system and their Protestant constitution was no more.[34]

In order for this to happen, the sole remaining major political disability – the ban on Catholics sitting in parliament – would have to be overcome. The agitation of this question for the first time in 1795 seemed initially to suggest that this would not be long delayed, but the refusal of the British government to countenance such a concession so long as Ireland retained a domestic parliament ensured that the strong Protestant opposition to the idea prevailed. Indeed, the capacity of conservative Protestants successfully to resist change increased in the years that followed as the polarisation of Irish politics between conservatives and radicals, and the reversal of the radical agenda with the failure of rebellion in 1798 boosted their numbers and influence. They were further aided by the invigoration during the same period of the ranks of British conservatism with the result that William Pitt, the prime minister, discovered to his dismay in 1801 that he was not able to deliver on the promise he made Irish Catholics at the time of the Union negotiations that Emancipation would soon follow.[35]

If this was a cruel set back for the hopes of Irish Catholics, who had supported the Act of Union in large numbers in the expectation of the early removal of the remaining Penal Laws, it was a matter of some satisfaction for those Protestants who were committed to the retention of the proscription on Catholics sitting in parliament. They were heartened further by the alliance they were enabled to forge thereafter with the forces of English conservatism, to which they made a vital ideological contribution, with the result that it became an axiom with many opponents of emancipation that the policy of conciliating Catholics by relaxing the Penal Laws was one of the primary causes of disorder in Ireland in the 1790s and that this constituted a direct threat to the political establishment as well as to law and order in Britain as well.[36] It proved a compelling argument to those who persisted in opposing every attempt to admit Catholics to the political process in the decades that followed.

Of course, everybody was not equally persuaded by the rhetoric of confessional constitutional exclusivity. Guided from 1805 by Henry Grattan, a nexus of liberal Irish Protestants joined with their British *confrères* in attempting to overcome the objections of their more numerous opponents. They contrived with some ingenuity to identify some middle ground that would satisfy all parties, but in vain. Their failure ensured that when Catholic emancipation was finally conceded in 1829 it was because primarily of the vigorous efforts of Catholics led by Daniel O'Connell, and because the alternative – a possible civil war in

Ireland and the fragmentation of the Anglo-Irish Union – was so much worse. More worrying still for the future, the primary legacy of the campaign and of the Penal Laws was one of acute denominational distrust that was to prove still more enduring.

V

Writing to Sir Robert Peel in March 1816, the historian and conservative Protestant ideologue Richard Musgrave observed with regret that because the Penal Laws against Catholics in Ireland were not imposed until a century after they were introduced in England and they were only allowed operate for seventy years, they were applied for too short a time to enable them to 'produce … the good effects which they did in England'.[37] This value-laden conclusion is not one that any historian today would endorse. However, any account of the introduction and operation of the Penal Laws would find less to disagree with Musgrave's observation that these laws were 'founded in political necessity and dictated by self-preservation' since this is how Protestants felt not just at the time of their enactment but, in the case of a majority of their number, for more than a century thereafter. This is why they offered such strong opposition to their repeal. The implications of this for the history of Christianity in Ireland is that the comforting assumption that the 'penal era' was short lived and was long over by the time Musgrave offered this observation is in need of reassessment. It attests also to the persistence of the fund of suspicion and intolerance that long sundered the members of the main Christian denominations, of which the Penal Laws remain a vivid symbol.

Notes
1. The term Penal Laws attained ascendancy in the nineteenth century. They were commonly termed the 'Popery laws' in the eighteenth.
2. M. A. Mullet, *Catholics in Britain and Ireland, 1558-1829,* Basingstoke 1998; John Miller, *Popery and Politics in England, 1660-1688,* Cambridge 1973.
3. Toby Barnard, *A New Anatomy of Ireland: The Irish Protestants, 1649-1770,* London 2002.

4. Raymond Gillespie, 'The Irish Protestants and James II, 1688-90', *Irish Historical Studies* 28 (1992), pp. 124-33.

5. See Bernadette Whelan (ed.), *The Last of the Great Wars: Essays on the War of the Three Kings in Ireland, 1688-91*, Limerick 1994.

6. James Kelly, 'Monitoring the constitution: Poynings' Law and the making of law in Ireland' (forthcoming).

7. ibid; Ivar McGrath, *The Making the Eighteenth-Century Irish Constitution*, Dublin 2000, chapter 3.

8. Maureen Wall, *The Penal Laws, 1691-1760* , Dundalk 1976.

9. Toby Barnard, 'Reforming Irish manners: the religious societies in Dublin during the 1690s', *Historical Journal* 35 (1992), pp 805-32.

10. Richard Caulfield (ed.), *Council Book of the Corporation of Cork*, Guildford 1876, pp. 266, 267, 319, 355; Sir John and Lady Gilbert (eds.), *Calendar of Ancient Records of Dublin* , 19 vols, Dublin 1889-1944, vi, pp. 379-80.

11. S. J. Connolly, *Religion, Law and Power: The Making of Protestant Ireland 1660-1760*, Oxford 1992, p. 263.

12. Caulfield (ed.), *Council Book of the Corporation of Cork*, pp. 239-40.

13. Colum Kenny, 'The exclusion of Catholics from the legal profession in Ireland', *Irish Historical Studies* 25 (1987), p. 352.

14. T. P. O'Neill, 'Discovers and discoveries: the Penal Laws and Dublin property', *Dublin Historical Record*, 37 (1981), pp 2-13.

15. For the Catholic church and repression see James Kelly, 'The impact of the Penal Laws' in James Kelly and Daire Keogh (eds.), *History of the Catholic diocese of Dublin*, Dublin 2000, pp 147-53; T. Hogan, 'Dr Patrick Donnelly, 1649-1716', *Seanchas Ardmhacha* 5 (1969), pp 18-20. Excellent insights into Catholic reaction can be gleaned from Cathaldus Giblin, (ed.), 'Catalogue of material of Irish interest in the collection Nunziatura di Fiandra parts 3 and 4', in *Collectanea Hibernica* 4 and 5 (1961-2).

16. See the petitions of Fr Paul Egan and John Browne, 1711-12 (British Library, Irish Petitions, Add. Ms 38160 ff 21, 48-9).

17. Proclamation, March 1713 (National Archives of Ireland).

18. Barnard, *A New Anatomy of Ireland*, p. 91.

19. Patrick Fagan, *An Irish Bishop in Penal Times: The Chequered Career of Sylvester Lloyd*, Dublin 1993, pp 47-52; Connolly, *Religion, Law and Power*, pp 282-4; Grafton to Cartaret, 15 Nov. 1723 (The National Archives [henceforth NA], SP63/382 f 18).

20. Patrick Fagan (ed.), *Ireland in the Stuart Papers* , 2 vols, Dublin 1995, i, 80; P. J. O'Connor, *Exploring Limerick's Past: An Historical Geography*, Newcastle West, 1987, p. 161.

21. Connolly, *Religion, Law and Power*, p. 284; F. G. James, *Lords of the ascendancy: the Irish House of Lords and its members, 1660-1800*, Dublin 1995, p. 138.

22. *Resolutions of the Lords Spiritual and Temporal in Parliament assembled upon the Present State of Popery in this Kingdom*, Dublin 1729, p. 1.

23. See, for examples, *Dublin Gazette*, 19 Dec. 1732, 13 April 1733; *Pue's Occurrences*, 7 August, 9 October 1739, 23 February 1748; *Dublin Courant*, 19 April, 26 July 1746, 10 December 1751, May 1756 passim.

24. Colin Haydon, *Anti-Catholicism in eighteenth-century England*, Manchester 1993; NA, PC2/91 ff 542, 571; PC2/92 ff 334, 337; PC2/98 ff 114, 139.

25. Quoted in Patrick Fagan, *Divided loyalties: the question of the oath for Irish Catholics in the eighteenth century*, Dublin 1997, p. 78; Bowes to Dodington, 21 April 1735 in HMC, *Reports on various collections, vi: Eyre Matcham Mss*, London 1909, p. 63.

26. Weston to Wilmot, 6 March 1750 (Public Record Office of Northern Ireland, T/3019/1504).

27. *The Letters of Lord Chief Baron Edward Willes to the Earl of Warwick, 1757-62*, ed., James Kelly, Aberystwyth 1990, p. 46; Thomas Power, 'Fr Nicholas Sheehy' in Gerard Moran (ed.), *Radical Irish Priests, 1660-1970* , Dublin 1998, pp. 62-78.

28. *Freeman's Journal*, 7 December 1765; Thomas Bartlett, *The Fall and Rise of the Irish Nation: The Catholic Question 1690-1830*, Dublin 1992, chapter 6.

29. *Gentleman's Magazine*, September 1763, p. 535.

30. Draft in Agar's handwriting of a Lords' protest, [17 December 1773] (PRONI, Normanton Papers, T/3719/M/5).

31. Bartlett, *The Fall and Rise of the Irish Nation*, chapter 6.

32. James Kelly, 'Parliamentary reform in Irish politics, 1760-90' in David Dickson et al (eds.), *The United Irishmen*, Dublin 1993, pp. 74-87.

33. James Kelly, 'The genesis of Protestant ascendancy' in Gerard O'Brien (ed.), *Parliament, politics and people*, Dublin 1987, pp 93-128.

34. James Kelly, 'Conservative Protestant political thought in late eighteenth-century Ireland' in S. J. Connolly (ed.), *Political ideas in eighteenth-century Ireland*, Dublin 2000, pp. 185-220.

35. Patrick Geoghegan, *The Irish Act of Union*, Dublin 1999, chapters 6 and 7.

36. Carleton to Redesdale, 30 September 1803 (British Library, Hardwicke Papers, Add. Ms 35742 ff 257-8). More generally, see James Sack, *From Jacobite to Conservative: reaction and orthodoxy in Britain, c. 1760-1830*, Cambridge 1993.

37. Musgrave to Peel, 5 March 1816 (British Library, Peel papers, Add. Ms 40253 ff 144-5).

Bibliography

Toby Barnard, *A new Anatomy of Ireland: the Irish Protestants, 1649-1770*, London 2002.

Thomas Bartlett, *The Fall and Rise of the Irish Nation The Catholic Question 1690-1830*, Dublin 1992.

S. J. Connolly, *Religion, Law and Power: The Making of Protestant Ireland 1660-1760*, Oxford 1992.

Patrick Fagan, *Divided loyalties: The Question of the Oath for Irish Catholics in the Eighteenth Century*, Dublin 1997.

Patrick Geoghegan, *The Irish Act of Union*, Dublin 1999.

Raymond Gillespie, 'The Irish Protestants and James II, 1688-90', *Irish Historical Studies* 28 (1992), pp 124-33.

Colin Haydon, *Anti-Catholicism in Eighteenth-Century England*, Manchester 1993.

James Kelly, 'The impact of the Penal Laws' in James Kelly and Dáire Keogh (eds.), *History of the Catholic Diocese of Dublin*, Dublin 2000.

James Kelly, 'Conservative Protestant political thought in late eighteenth-century Ireland' in S. J. Connolly (ed.), *Political ideas in Eighteenth-Century Ireland*, Dublin 2000, pp 185-220.

M. A. Mullet, *Catholics in Britain and Ireland, 1558-1829*, Basingstoke 1998.

T. P. O'Neill, 'Discovers and discoveries: the Penal Laws and Dublin property', *Dublin Historical Record* 37 (1981), pp 2-13.

James Sack, *From Jacobite to Conservative: Reaction and Orthodoxy in Britain, c. 1760-1830*, Cambridge 1993.

Maureen Wall, *The Penal Laws, 1691-1760*, Dundalk 1976.

Delivered 14 May 2002

Churches and Theology in a Century of Revolution and Reaction[1]

A. R. Pierce

Characterising the churches' experience over the course of a century is, of necessity, an exercise in simplification and caricature. Such caricature may be forgiven, however, insofar as it kick-starts serious engagement with the ideas and institutions that shaped those complex creatures – the men, women and children who lived and died only a few generations ago, yet who seem more alien to us the more we know of them. When early nineteenth-century thinkers looked back at the preceding century to caricature their forbears, they chose – with conscious irony – to label it 'the Age of Reason', and the name stuck. What interpretative label is evoked by a period that was, until only recently, the century before our own? And, in choosing a label, we are seeking to cast light on how the churches understood their role in a century which witnessed Bonaparte and Victoria, Marxism and colonialism, famine and urban expansion, religious revivalism and popular expressions of religious doubt, Pius IX – *Pio Nono* – and popular anticlericalism, ultramontanism and social democracy.

In his recent Gifford Lectures, the critic George Steiner observed that:

> Roughly from the time of Waterloo to that of the massacres on the Western front in 1915-16, the European bourgeoisie experienced a privileged season, an armistice with history. Underwritten by the exploitation of industrial labour at home and colonial rule abroad, Europeans knew a century of progress, of liberal dispensations, of reasonable hope.[2]

Unlike most historical eras – particularly our own – Steiner views the nineteenth century as the era in which the West be-

lieved in 'progress'. It is certainly true that many writers of this
period viewed themselves – and Western, Christian culture in
general – as being on a progressive and civilising mission towards the rest of the world. 'Progress' impacts in two directions
at once: it is directed towards a glorious future, and this orient-
ation implies a negative judgement on the past and the present,
both of which may be neglected or downgraded in the drive to
achieve progress. Some of the century's more sensitive souls –
John Henry Newman (1801-1890) and Søren Kierkegaard (1813-
1855), for example – offered alternative verdicts on the authority
of past and present respectively: but the gloom that encircled
Newman, as well as that which Baron Friedrich von Hügel
(1852-1925) detected in Kierkegaard (whom he dubbed the
'gloomy Dane') was out of kilter with the culture of the industri-
alised West, apart from pockets of resistance offered by recur-
rent Romanticism.

Hence, the nineteenth century witnessed a dramatic and continuous oscillation between revolutionary movements, eager to
effect rapid change, and reactionary movements that viewed
change as betrayal. Each set of movements directed its affections
towards a golden age, yet disagreed with the other on the location of that golden age: must we return to the past, as the
Romantics believed in their glorification of medieval Europe?
Or do we set our faces to an allegedly scientific future, as continental positivists like Auguste Comte (1798-1857) believed?

This interplay of revolution and reaction is evident in most
Western countries in the nineteenth century – including Ireland
– but perhaps its clearest manifestation occurs in France, which
lurched from monarchy to mob in 1789 (the date that many cultural historians see as the start of the nineteenth century), and
which continued to experience ideological ping-pong throughout the century, as monarchists and republicans disputed the
ideal political arrangements for the eldest daughter of the
Western church.

A sea-change in religion's social role

For the western churches in general, the nineteenth century proved unsettling. The preceding century had been no less difficult, but its impact was restricted in scope. Enlightenment *philosophes* had, indeed, subjected revealed religion to prolonged dips in the acid baths of critical reason but, as Owen Chadwick has noted, Enlightenment was for the few, whereas the increasingly secularised worldview of the nineteenth century was available to the many.[3]

An understanding of relations between the few and the many, and of the social structures that govern them, has grown increasingly prominent in the efforts of cultural historians to interpret the actions and reactions of the European churches in the period under consideration. One illuminating approach is taken by the French historian of ideas, Marcel Gauchet, who has attended to changes in the *social function* of religion to a greater extent than is usual in historical theology.[4] For most of its history, the Christian religion, like the religions it displaced, functioned as a structural element of society, holding together society with a cohesive power like no other contemporary social institution. Napoleon Bonaparte, for example, may not have been up to speed on his catechism, but he appreciated the role of religion in holding the fabric of society together – he did not care particularly which church was involved. Closer to home, the social role of religion is underlined by the terms of the Act of Union in 1801, in which political union implied the incorporation of the Church of Ireland into the United Church of England and Ireland: to the premodern political imagination, Establishment and religion presupposed one another.

From the eighteenth century on, according to Gauchet, and fuelled by secularising tendencies derived from within the Judaeo-Christian tradition, the social role of religion began to change, and the churches found themselves compelled – in most cases reluctantly – to discern a new social role for themselves in a disenchanted, modern world. (An obvious, though hardly radical, example is the end of the Church of Ireland's established status in 1870.) Religion had become an area of life in which members of society could exercise choice: it was no longer a structural element of society. Modernity began to emerge as the cultural climate to which the churches would have to adjust: the sociologist Peter Berger describes this quintessentially modern experience as a move from religious identity as a matter of fate to religious identity as a matter of choice.[5]

Gauchet's thesis is borne out by a consideration of the Oxford Movement in the Church of England, one of the pivotal developments within modern Anglican self-understanding, and which is still charged with ecumenical repercussions. A number of Oxford dons, led by John Henry Newman and John Keble (1792-1866), grew alarmed at the way in which government policy seemed, to their eyes, less than respectful towards the theological integrity of the established church. The Reform Bill of 1832, and especially a proposal the following year to suppress 10 bishoprics in the Church of Ireland, brought matters to a head: was the established church the mystical reality of Christ's body militant here in earth? Or, was it merely one more government body, to be adjusted in the interests of political expediency and without reference to theological considerations? The suppression of Irish bishoprics was attacked by John Keble in a famous sermon of July 1833 as an act of 'National Apostasy.' For Newman and his colleagues, who let fly a series of *Tracts for the Times*, the principal issue concerned the catholicity of the Church of England and Ireland, and its continuity with the church of Christ's apostles. The *Tracts* urged that the church was to be understood – and treated – as a divine gift, and not instrumentalised in the interests of the temporal power. Whilst the rationale for the Oxford Movement may have been presented – and contested – primarily in theological terms, its impact demonstrates Gauchet's point: after the eighteenth century, religion was increasingly disentangling itself (or finding itself being disentangled) from the post-Constantinian alliances of throne and altar which had characterised medieval Europe. It is both banal and characteristically modern to note that there is something distinctively *religious* about religious institutions. The emerging challenge for the churches was that of articulating this irreducible religiousness whilst retaining critical awareness of the fragility and contingency of the cultural and social forms (doctrine, polity, political engagement with wider society, etc.) inhabited to date by faith and culture.

'Liberalism' in the Church

When Newman received his red hat in 1879 from Pope Leo XIII, he claimed that the unifying feature of his life, as a priest in both the Church of England and in the Roman Catholic Church, had been his opposition to 'liberalism'. This, Newman idiosyncratically defined as the anti-dogmatic religious principle. Ironically, to many in authority in the Roman Catholic Church at the time (including other converts from Anglicanism like Manning and Faber), Newman, far from opposing liberalism, appeared as its very incarnation and, until the pontificate of Leo, Newman – and he was not alone in this – found the church of Pius IX to be a cold, inhospitable *unam sanctam*.

Liberalism – like conservatism – is a much-abused word. During the nineteenth century, however, it became an important term in both theology and church politics, with the label 'Liberal Protestantism' coined to describe those Protestant theologians (usually German) who, in the tradition of Friedrich Schleiermacher (1763-1834), attempted to reinterpret Christianity to post-Enlightenment culture and society.

Painfully aware that an allegedly traditional orthodoxy appeared increasingly incomprehensible to a new generation shaped by the post-Enlightenment Romantic movement, Schleiermacher insisted that what his contemporaries (the 'cultured despisers' of religion) were rejecting as religion, was not in fact religion at all. Religion, he argued, was essentially a matter of experience – and not, therefore, essentially a matter of metaphysics or morals. The key term is essence: religion in general, and the Christian religion in particular, embodied an unchanging essence, namely, the felt experience of utter dependence, which had generated secondary expressions of that experience in scripture, doctrine and history, but, without due attention to its experiential roots, the scriptural and doctrinal by-products of religious experience were simply 'dead embers'.[6] As the metaphor of 'embers' suggests, Schleiermacher did not ignore past expressions of religious experience: embers, after all, indicate fires that had once burned. Hence, many of his followers turned their attention to these 'embers', and achieved prominence in biblical and doctrinal history as they interrogated the texts and traditions of Christianity to see how its essence had been interpreted at different times and in different cultures in the past.

History as the presence of a different past
To refer to the past as being 'different' to the present highlights another issue with which the churches struggled in the nineteenth century, namely the extraordinary invigoration provided by the discipline of history, leading to an emphasis on the 'otherness' of the past, together with a growing sense of discontinuity between past and present. For an historic religion like Christianity, in which religious and historical truth claims intermingle, the idea of a conflict between religious faith and critical history was potentially disquieting, to say the least. Precisely such a conflict had been anticipated in the writings of Gotthold Ephraim Lessing (1729-81), one of the key figures in the German Enlightenment, and a major influence on subsequent Liberal Protestant theology. Perhaps best known for his dictum 'the accidental truths of history can never become the proof of necessary truths of reason,' Lessing's historical researches led him to discover an 'ugly ditch' between the findings of the historians and the claims of religious dogma.

The problem was not simply a matter of the difference between faith and historical inquiry – history deals in probabilities, whereas religious faith prefers to attribute something more than probability to its truth claims.[7] The problem of history, as it presented itself to the churches in the nineteenth century was less subtle. Protestant theologians tended to describe the problem as the relationship between faith and history, Catholic theologians preferred to talk of the relationship between history and dogma. But the basic problem was felt in each tradition, and it was expressed memorably in George and Ira Gershwin's *Porgy and Bess:*

De t'ings dat yo' li'ble to read in de Bible
It ain't necessarily so.

Treating the Bible like any other ancient text, 'higher critics' sought to establish the historical reliability of the biblical texts, using other ancient texts and archaeology to assist them. The biblical text was treated as a window onto the ancient world, through which we might gain some insight into the world in which these texts came to be written, collected and edited. The compelling aim of situating the biblical texts in their historical context had the paradoxical affect of alienating some within the churches, because the findings of these methods invariably sounded subversive to those who had been encouraged to read and to learn their bibles: Abraham was mythical rather than historical, Moses did not write the Pentateuch, the text of Ecclesiastes had been cheered-up by a marginally less depressed editor, the Infancy Narratives are theological reflections not gynaecological case studies. And so on.

For many religious readers, the historical treatment of sacred history proved shocking, and it raised difficult questions concerning the way in which these texts could be regarded as divinely inspired. Donald Charlton captures the mood of many in the nineteenth century, when he writes of 'the religious temperament estranged from the Christian faith'.[8] Certainly religious doubt emerged as one of the major themes in contemporary literature: consider the agonies endured by Mrs Humphrey Ward's hero *Robert Elsmere* (1888), or an earlier lament for the ages of faith found in Matthew Arnold's 'Dover Beach' (1867). Arnold's closing lines acknowledge with bitter wistfulness the scale of disenchantment:

The Sea of Faith
Was once, too, at the full, and round earth's shore
Lay like the folds of a bright girdle furled.
But now I only hear
Its melancholy, long, withdrawing roar,
Retreating, to the breath
Of the night-wind, down to the vast edges drear
And naked shingles of the world.[9]

Learning to live with the past

How were the churches to negotiate a way across Lessing's 'ugly ditch' between safe historical judgement on the one side, and doctrinal truth claims on the other? One idea came from Schleiermacher and was employed by other prominent Liberal Protestants such as Albrecht Ritschl (1822-1889) and Adolf von Harnack (1851-1930), namely the idea of Christianity's 'essence'. Initially intended as a defence against those who found Christianity intellectually weak, the notion of Christianity's essence also provided a suitable tool for accounting for *both* continuity and discontinuity in church history. This was important for Protestant church historians, who needed to show that there was continuity between Protestantism now and the apostolic church then, as well as discontinuity between medieval Catholicism and reformers like Luther and Calvin. For Liberal Protestants, therefore, Christianity's essence could account for Christianity's movement through history – sometimes the essence was more evident (e.g. in Liberal Protestantism), and sometimes nearly smothered by its context (e.g. in Roman Catholicism). The predictability of these examples highlights the extent to which church history, as a discipline, remained an apologetical instrument of denominationally-constricted nineteenth century theology.

John Henry Newman did not appreciate talk of Christianity's essence, or 'leading idea,' which, he believed, would simplify – and therefore distort – the historical reality of Christianity.[10] Newman's conversion to Roman Catholicism in 1845 coincided with the publication of his classic work, *An Essay on the*

Development of Doctrine.[11] As an Anglican and as an historian, Newman had grown increasingly dissatisfied with the lip-service paid by Anglicans to the allegedly normative status of the primitive church, usually regarded as the first five centuries. But why five? Why not six, or seven or eight? How does one make a *theological* judgement that the first five centuries provide doctrinal purity, when, as an *historian* it is simply not possible to spot the sudden deluge of doctrinal contamination in the early sixth century? Moreover, the church of the first five centuries bore a disturbing lack of resemblance to the nineteenth century Church of England: the early Fathers showed much less relish than Newman's contemporaries in discoursing on Original Sin, they referred doctrinal questions to the see of Rome, and their liturgical life invoked Mary the Mother of God and the other saints with more enthusiasm than would have been safe for a Church of England priest in Newman's day.

To avoid special pleading, Newman chose not to select one period of church history and declare it alone to be especially authoritative. Newman was seeking a way to appeal to the church's history as a totality, which he interpreted as the explicating of an original 'idea'. This process of explication was what Newman called the development of doctrine.

Today, talk of doctrinal development has become commonplace, and it is hard to realise the extent to which Newman's proposal was genuinely shocking at the time. Surely the church had always taught what it now taught? Hence the Latin tag *semper eadem* ('always the same') to describe the content of the faith. But acknowledging doctrinal development carried a consquence for Newman which led him out of Anglicanism: it was, he argued 'antecedently probable' that God had given to the world an infallible interpreter – i.e. the magisterium of the Roman Catholic Church – to guard against doctrinal corruption.

Thus, Protestant liberals saw the essence of Christianity making erratic progress (that word again) through history, and Roman Catholics with a sense for history, like Newman, perceived doctrinal continuity guaranteed by development occurring in a church infallibly guided through the vicissitudes of history.

Tradition and the manufacture of doctrinally-correct history
If the appeal to history was causing loss of sleep to some of the nineteenth century's more sensitive souls, the appeal to tradition – by contrast – was thriving. These two appeals – to history and to tradition – were bound to collide, particularly when historians began to ask impolite questions about the parentage of certain traditions. Twentieth century historians – especially Eric Hobsbawm and Terence Ranger – have highlighted the extent of nineteenth century inventiveness in the manufacture of traditions.[12] Hobsbawm and Ranger were primarily concerned with aspects of cultural history with dubious claims to being 'traditional,' e.g. the kilt as popular Scottish dress, or Morris dancing as a venerable English pastime. Clearly our need for roots will be satisfied, even if we have to go to the trouble of inventing them. But the same drive to invent tradition can be detected in nineteenth-century church life and, in particular, in ways in which certain groups within the churches defined themselves as spokespersons for 'traditional orthodoxy'. Viewed historically, however, such groups are anything but traditional – they have novelty writ large upon themselves. Biblicist movements of the nineteenth century provide a good example.

Arguably, the most significant feature of recent religious and cultural history is the emergence of 'fundamentalism'. From its origins in American Evangelical Protestantism in the early twentieth century, the term has been applied to analogous developments within other Christian traditions and in other religions (notably Islam, particularly since the 1979 coup in Iran). Even if the term fundamentalism did not first appear in the nineteenth century, its prior enabling conditions may be discerned there in embryonic form.

All religious traditions live with compromises and constant tensions between their conservative and their progressive constituencies, and whilst on first inspection fundamentalism may appear as a conservative movement, it is more accurate to re-gard it as a modern anti-modernism. It is defined by its rejection of a modernism, often a 'modernism' that it has defined in order to reject, and certainly not modernity *simpliciter*. Some nine-teenth century movements, for example, Catholic Traditionalism in France or the doctrine of theopneustia taught by Louis Gaussen (1790-1863) at Geneva, anticipate some of the concerns that would later develop into fully-fledged fundamentalisms – but they are still epistemological strategies for security in a post-Cartesian world, and not yet fundamentalist rejections of a mod-ernism.

The Old Testament writer of Ecclesiastes – if he existed – thought that there was nothing new under the sun. By the end of the nineteenth century, thoughtful Christians were beginning to suspect that there was nothing old there either.

Conclusion

Of all scholarly summaries of the nineteenth century, Joseph Fitzer's *précis* of scientific development is the most pithy: 'trains, Darwin, vaccination and Freud'.[13] The eighteenth century had taken a positive view of the human person, as a reasonable, vir-tuous individual, whose rationality made possible real choice and therefore real morality. By the end of the nineteenth century, this virtuous individual was in deep trouble. Charles Darwin (1809-1882) had demonstrated our species' continuity with the rest of nature. Victorians – who enjoyed collecting wild animals – now found that a trip to the Zoo provided a chance to visit some disturbingly close cousins in the primates' house. Trains had made mass-mobility a reality, and with that mobility came new and unsettling ideas – successive popes had resisted the in-troduction of railways into the papal states, fearing the onset of democratic ideas. Vaccination – like other public health schemes – had begun to impact on the size of the population, and danger-ous ideas about eugenics were starting to circulate. Finally, Sigmund Freud (1856-1939) did for the interior reality of the human person what Karl Marx (1818-1883) had done for society:

from Marx we had learned that we are products of economic forces largely beyond our control. According to Freud, we are much less rational than we think we are: our sense of self conceals a battle to control the impulsive, irrational, id; our moral sense and our conscience – on which eighteenth century divinity had been apt to dilate – are merely the dictates of superego.

By 1914, evidence in support of Freud appeared to hand, and the age of progress was ready to go over the top. At the time, a young Protestant theologian, Karl Barth (1886-1968), observed with horror as Christian theology (embodied in the actions of his professors) colluded in the madness of war, and he set about a radical appraisal of the path taken by theology through the nineteenth century. The Barthian reaction against Liberal Protestantism coincided with the drive of Pope Pius X to eradicate the heresy of 'modernism' from the Roman Catholic Church, as defined and condemned in the encyclical *Pascendi dominici gregis* (1907). Meanwhile, on the far side of the Atlantic, in 1910, the first volumes of *The Fundamentals* were published in defence of an allegedly imperiled orthodoxy, thereby providing a name for a movement of enduring significance.

At the dawn of the nineteenth century, religion had been on the defensive in post-Enlightenment Europe; as it ended, however, offensive religion was staging a comeback.

Notes

1. George Steiner, *Grammars of Creation*, Faber, London 2001, p. 2.
2. Owen Chadwick, *The Secularization of the European Mind in the Nineteenth Century*, Cambridge University Press, Cambridge 1995.
3. Marcel Gauchet, *Le Désenchantement du monde: une histoire politique de la religion*, Gallimard, Paris 1985; ET *The Disenchantment of the World: A Political History of Religion*, translated by Oscar Burge, foreword by Charles Taylor, Princeton University Press, Princeton NJ 1997.
4. Peter L. Berger, *The Heretical Imperative: Contemporary Possibilities of Religious Affirmation*, Doubleday, New York 1979, 11-17.
5. Friedrich Schleiermacher, *On Religion: Speeches to its Cultured Despisers*, Introduction, translation and notes by Richard Crouter, Texts in German Philosophy, Cambridge University Press, Cambridge 1988.
6. The theologian who probed most deeply into the implications of the conflict between historical and dogmatic methods was Ernst Troeltsch (1865-1923).

7. Donald Charlton, *Secular Religions in France 1815-1870*, University of Hull, London 1963, p. 4.

8. Matthew Arnold, 'Dover Beach', in J. Wain (ed.), *The Oxford Anthology of English Poetry, vol 2: Blake to Heaney, 1986*, Oxford: Oxford University Press, 2005, 455-6.

9. On the contesting of Christianity's 'essence', see Stephen Sykes, *The Identity of Christianity: Theologians and the Essence of Christianity from Schleiermacher to Barth*, SPCK, London 1984.

10. John Henry Newman, *An Essay on the Development of Christian Doctrine*, The Edition of 1845, Edited with an introduction by J.M.Cameron, Penguin Books, Harmondsworth 1974.

11. See the informative and amusing account provided in Eric Hobsbawm and Terence Ranger, (eds.), *The Invention of Tradition*, Cambridge University Press, Cambridge 1983.

12. Joseph Fitzer, ed., *Romance and the Rock: Nineteenth-Century Catholics on Faith and Reason*, Fortress Texts in Modern Theology, Fortress Press, Minneapolis, p. 5.

Select Bibliography

Karl Barth, *Protestant Theology in the Nineteenth Century*, 1952, ET, SCM Press, London 2001.

J. W. Burrow, *The Crisis of Reason: European Thought, 1848-1914*, Yale University Press, New Haven and London 2000.

B. A. Gerrish, *The Old Protestantism and the New: Essays on the Reformation Heritage*, T. & T. Clark, Edinburgh1982.

Martin E. Marty and R. Scott Appleby, *The Fundamentalism Project*, 5 vols., University of Chicago Press, Chicago and London 1991-95.

Alec R Vidler, *The Church in an Age of Revolution: 1789 to the Present Day*, Pelican History of the Church 5, 1961; Penguin Books, Harmondsworth 1974.

James A. Winders, *European Culture Since 1848: From Modern to Postmodern and Beyond*, Palgrave, New York and Basingstoke 2001.

First delivered under the title 'The nineteenth century: revolution and reform' on 21 May 2002, and later published as 'The church in the nineteenth century: revolution and reaction', in Search: A Church of Ireland Journal 25, 2 (2002), 123-130

The Irish Church in the Twentieth and Twenty-first Centuries

Ferdinand von Prondzynski

Introduction

The previous lectures in this series have all been given by noted historians or church historians, and they have provided their listeners with some detailed and learned insights into the various periods and movements of church history. I cannot claim any such expertise myself, so what you will be getting from me today will be more in the nature of a polemic. In any case, half of my subject lies in the future, so I shall be able to overcome my lack of detailed knowledge with speculation – which may in any case be more fun.

I shall however try to distil some broader themes from my subject-matter. These themes will be the following:

1. *The churches and tribalism.* To what extent could it be said that the churches became religious societies whose major identity lay not in their theology but in their support for particular groupings within the Irish nation?

2. *The churches and morals.* To what extent have the churches been able to influence (for good or otherwise) public ethics and morals?

3. *The churches and ecumenism.* To what extent have the churches harnessed the potential for development provided by the ecumenical movement?

4. *The churches and faith.* To what extent have the churches been able to maintain and communicate a clear faith to their members, in the context of a major decline in religious belief in the western world?

From these themes I shall try to draw some conclusions expressing where the church in Ireland may be going over the next century, and where I believe it ought to go if it is to be true to its mission of communicating the gospel and if it is to be successful in this mission.

The churches and tribalism

Very close to the beginning of my period, in 1907, Pope Pius X promulgated the *Ne Temere Decree*, which provided that in marriages between Catholics and non-Catholics the rules of the Roman Catholic church were to apply to the forms and consequences of marriage; this produced an unequal relationship between the denominations in such marriages. The Decree was followed by sharp rejoinders from a variety of Protestant churchmen, including one from the then Rector of Blackrock in Cork, John Allen Fitzgerald Gregg (later to be Archbishop of Dublin and Archbishop of Armagh). The state of mind in which Gregg delivered his denunciation of *Ne Temere* was described a little later by his daughter:

> The arrogance of [the RC church] enraged him, the claim that it alone was the true church, when by contrast with the Eastern Orthodox church it was the Roman church which was schismatic. The wickedness of the *Ne Temere* decree outraged his sense of justice and fair play.

Gregg in fact was a notable and celebrated advocate of theological Catholicism within the Anglican tradition, but his reaction illustrated what was to become a major feature of the twentieth century: the struggle between the churches to assert themselves as representatives of a particular tradition in Ireland. This scene was complicated further by the divisions within the Protestant parts of the church, which often helped to escalate the language of confrontation between different theological and national viewpoints.

We shall be looking in a moment at the way in which the ecumenical movement affected this scene, but that came rather later.

The inherent tribalism of the time created particular pressures within the Church of Ireland. These found an interesting expression in the doctrinal and ritual controversies surrounding a small number of priests in the church in the first half of the century. I want to focus briefly on two of these.

The first concerned the Vicar of St Bartholomew's Church, Canon Walter Simpson. Canon Simpson was accused in 1928 by four petitioners of having committed at least ten breaches of the rubrics then in force, and these violations included:

i. During the administration of the Holy Communion, standing at the West Side of the Holy Table.

ii. Bowing to the Holy Table on several occasions during Divine Service.

iii. Making the sign of the cross when placing the alms upon the Holy Table.

iv. At Evening Prayer, immediately before the Magnificat, using a Hymn, called by him the Office Hymn.

v. Carrying a Cross and allowing and permitting persons to do so through the Church in a Procession as a Rite or Ceremony.

The case was heard before the Court of the General Synod, and Canon Simpson was found guilty and fined £220.

A similar case was taken in 1935 against the Revd S. R. S. Colquhoun, Vicar of the Church of St John the Evangelist, Sandymount – a case which was also taken through the civil courts as Fr Colquhoun, unsuccessfully, tried to stop the church proceedings. The case against Fr Colquhoun included the following:

i. That he said the Lord's Prayer inaudibly at the beginning of the Service of Holy Communion.

ii. That he made the sign of the Cross during the Ascription before the sermon, and when pronouncing the Absolution.

iii. That he caused a bell to be rung during the Manual Acts at the Prayer of Consecration.

iv. That he sang or caused to be sung the Agnus Dei.

v. That 'during the said service [he] did wear a Biretta which he frequently removed from or replaced on his head, and also wore a cope or a chasuble and other ecclesiastical vestments or ornaments not prescribed or permitted by the canons'.

Fr Colquhoun was also found guilty and fined.

The complaints in these cases were of course perfectly proper in the sense that what was complained of was illegal under the rules of the Church of Ireland. Nevertheless, it raises the question as to why these rules existed and why they were enforced. They represented in the real sense a tribal identification of the Church of Ireland as a church that was not Roman Catholic – a way of judging what was right by refusing to accept what the other church did. While the twentieth century saw some changes adopted to these rules, a good few of the complaints made against the two clergymen would be valid complaints today. What is interesting (and I shall return to this) is that there would be no shortage of potential violators today, and by and large we do not see petitioners emerging to move against them.

The tribal instincts were in the twentieth century underpinned by political events. From the Easter Rising and the War of Independence, through the creation of the Irish Free State, through the development of the political culture of Northern Ireland, through the trade war with Britain, through the tensions of the Second World War, through the Northern Ireland 'Troubles', events pitted Catholics against Protestants and persuaded them to call on their churches to back their political causes. The churches by and large have done so. Their leaders have called for restraint when extremism appeared, but on the whole they have identified with these political groupings. The effect has been traumatic at times, as for example in the case of the 1981 hunger strikes in the Maze prison or in the case of Drumcree.

The churches and morals

One battleground for the tribal warfare has been in the area of public morals. All mainstream churches have made attempts during the last century to assert moral rules and values, although it must also be said that they have not covered a wide spectrum of ethics. The main flashpoint has been in the area of sexual morality, an area that became interesting in this setting as science and commerce made possible new lifestyles for the wider population. In responding to these changes, the churches on the whole tried to restrain them and to assert in the political arena the right to do so.

One of the more dramatic illustrations of the latter phenomenon was the response by the Roman Catholic church to the Mother and Child Health Plan, proposed in the early 1950s by the then Minister for Health, Dr Noel Browne. This plan envisaged the provision of pre- and post-natal care to mothers and medical care to children up to the age of 16. This was vehemently opposed by the Catholic church, which argued that the state had no competence in these areas. The bishops sent a letter to the Government, which read in part:

> The powers taken by the State in the proposed Mother and Child health service are in direct opposition to the rights of the family and of the individual and are liable to very great abuse. Their character is such that no assurance that they would be used in moderation could justify their enactment. If adopted they would constitute a ready-made instrument for totalitarian aggression.

The Cabinet as a result would not support the Minister, with the then Taoiseach declaring in the Dáil that he was 'an Irishman second, and a Catholic first'.

The same struggle between the church and the emerging claim for independence by the state recurred in the constitutional referendum campaigns of the 1980s. By now this was also a tribal setting, as the Protestant churches by and large adopted an opposing position on the issues of divorce and the inclusion within the constitution of a ban on abortion.

The churches and ecumenism

Nevertheless, throughout this time there was also the development of ecumenism, encouraged in particular by the Second Vatican Council and its emphasis on inter-church reconciliation. In the early 1960s it was still more or less unknown for Catholics and Protestants to attend services in each other's churches.

Prelates from each side tended to meet on various occasions, but rarely to discuss matters of common interest or joint initiatives. It was still forbidden to Catholics to go to Trinity College, and very few Protestants would attend any other university.

A major change was brought about by the Second Vatican Council's *Decree on Ecumenism*, which stated amongst other things:

All who have been 'justified by faith in baptism' are members of the Body of Christ; they all have the right to be called Christian; the children of the Catholic Church accept them as brothers.

And also:

Catholics are encouraged to join in ecumenical activity, and to meet non-Catholic Christians in truth and love.

The explosion of ecumenism changed a good deal of the cosmetics, but whether it penetrated the real areas of theological principle is another matter. Recent disagreements over the matter of intercommunion demonstrate the great fragility of inter-denominational co-operation and partnership. This is so despite the significant strides made by each side in edging a little closer to the other's point of view. In the early twentieth century, the idea of the 'Real Presence' of Christ in the Eucharist was dismissed as erroneous at a Church of Ireland Synod. By the end of the century, it is generally accepted in Anglicanism, while the Roman Catholic view of transubstantiation (at least as expounded by some leading theologians post-Vatican II) seems to be indistinguishable in practice from the idea of the Real Presence.

In all of this, major contributions were made by the Anglican-Roman Catholic International Commission (ARCIC), the first phase of which was co-chaired by Archbishop Henry McAdoo.

The churches and faith

While all these tensions were being revealed between the main-stream churches, a wholly different tide was sweeping through the wider society. Just before the beginning of the twentieth century, the following sermon was preached by an Anglican parish priest in an urban London parish for the Harvest Thanksgiving service:

Today you see in this church apples and pears, carrots and potatoes, wheat and barley. They are the fruits of the harvest, for which we offer thanks to Almighty God. God, in His mercy, works great miracles, and in His kindness clothes us and feeds us.

But there are other miracles. We have the railways, which take us at previously unimaginable speeds to places we could never have known, over great bridges and viaducts which defy nature. There is iron and steel. There are great machines, which work mysteriously and mightily. These are all miracles as well, and miracles which perhaps will touch the people of this city much more than the ploughshare and the sheaths of corn. And some will say they are not God's miracles at all, but the miracles wrought by our scientists and engineers. In this church we say weekly that God became man. Others say and think that, with our factories and our industry, man has become God.

Much of the period since then has seen the churches struggle, usually unsuccessfully, with the contention that their message, at any rate when delivered in biblical language without additional interpretation, had become irrelevant. The great social movements became secular (with some exceptions), and the churches' congregations began to drift away.

There have been largely two responses to this, in my view both seriously wrong. The first is to suppose that the departing public wanted greater theological certainties, best delivered in uncompromising fundamentalist language – although sometimes mediated through modern idiom in language and music. The second response has been to throw in the towel on the bible and the creeds and to reinterpret the Christian message to suit the supposed spirit of the times.

The fundamentalist response is sometimes admired by church people for its ability to fill some churches, often with the aid of charismatic emotion. But these successes have probably merely moved people within the spectrum of churchgoing – there is little evidence that they have even slightly stemmed the tide of departure. The liberal theological approach, encouraged by major church figures such as David Jenkins, Jack Spong, and the Sea of Faith and Jesus Seminar theologians, has some intellectual appeal but does little to attract larger groups of the faithful.

The Jesus Seminar provides an interesting insight into the nature of the debate. It was established in 1985, and in a programme of research lasting until 1996 the theologians involved concluded that, in their view, around 18 per cent of the biblical accounts of acts done by Jesus were historically accurate. This theme was picked up also by Jack Spong, former Bishop of Newark, who published 12 theses on Christianity in 1998. Some of these read as follows:

Theism, as a way of defining God, is dead. So most theological God-talk is today meaningless. A new way to speak of God must be found.

Since God can no longer be conceived in theistic terms, it becomes nonsensical to seek to understand Jesus as the incarnation of the theistic deity. So the Christology of the ages is bankrupt.

The virgin birth, understood as literal biology, makes Christ's Divinity, as traditionally understood, impossible.

The miracle stories of the New Testament can no longer be interpreted … as supernatural events performed by an incarnate deity.

The view of the cross as the sacrifice for the sins of the world is a barbarian idea based on primitive concepts of God and must be dismissed.

These contributions to the debate about the meaning of Christianity present a religion and a faith which is unrecognisable to many members of the church.

Set against this drift is the fundamentalism of others. The evangelical organisation Reform, for example, states that it was formed to react against the 'loss of confidence in the truth and power of the gospel' seen in mainstream Anglicanism. In a statement of its key aims, Reform Ireland emphasises its 'renewed belief and confidence in the inspiration, infallibility and inerrancy of Scripture as the final authority for Christian faith and practice'.

The churches therefore face a growing chasm within their own ranks, as some theologians and clergy assert a wholly new form of Christianity (and occasionally, as in the case of Dean Furlong, a new form of non-Christian religion), while others seek to row back the general drift of theological scholarship to some basic fundamental certainties. Both sides, by the way, have an uneasy relationship with science, which neither group seems fully to understand.

It is not necessarily surprising that this difference has not been capable of easy reconciliation, and that the churches are not finding it easy to declare a coherent message to their faithful. Some regard such absence of uniformity a strength; but measured in terms of organisational capacity and growth it almost certainly is not.

Into the future

As we move into the twenty-first century, the churches face huge challenges and contradictions. For much of the twentieth century the debates within and between the churches still mattered in Ireland, and the great social dilemmas and changes were fashioned or at least influenced by the churches.

At the beginning of the twenty-first century this is no longer so. There is no great evidence that people are still interested in what the church may wish to tell us about lifestyles, and there is a good deal of evidence that the focus on such issues serves to turn away those whose faith is no longer secure. There is no evidence that the churches' moves to make themselves 'relevant' by liturgical innovation strikes much of a chord (and I say this as a supporter of some forms of innovation). There is no evidence that church leaders can count on deference or respect any more.

However, there is evidence that the church can still provide comfort in times of great national or international stress. There is evidence that religious belief is still widespread, even if it is usually alarmingly vague in content. There is evidence that the churches' message on public ethics and standards of conduct would be listened to if it were declared in a more determined manner. Religion, as R. H. Tawney wrote in the early twentieth century, must stop being 'an ornament of leisure rather than the banner of a crusade'.

The main inhibitor of a still thriving church must now be the various denominations' tribal history. It seems to me to be time that the Church of Ireland in particular should cease to see itself as a 'Protestant' church, and that it should concentrate instead on its future as a reformed catholic church. In doing so, it would actually be developing the mission favoured by its former twentieth-century Primate, Archbishop Gregg.

Delivered on 27 May 2002

The Contributors

Editors

John R. Bartlett	Fellow Emeritus, Trinity College, Dublin
Stuart D. Kinsella	Research Adviser, Culture Committee, Christ Church Cathedral, Dublin

Contributors

Seán Freyne	Former Professor of Theology, and Fellow Emeritus of Trinity College, Dublin
Michael Haren	Editor of the *Calendar of Papal Registers*, Irish Manuscripts Commission
Catherine Swift	Lecturer in Irish Studies, Mary Immaculate College, University of Limerick
Howard Clarke	Former Associate Professor of Medieval Socio-Economic History, University College, Dublin
Marie-Therese Flanagan	Senior Lecturer, School of History and Anthropology, The Queen's University, Belfast
Bernadette Williams	Formerly of the Department of Medieval History, Trinity College, Dublin
Colm Lennon	Associate Professor, Department of History, National University of Ireland, Maynooth
James Kelly	Head of Department of History, St Patrick's College, Drumcondra
Andrew Pierce	Lecturer in Ecumenical Studies and Coordinator of the Ecumenical Studies Programme, Irish School of Ecumenics (Trinity College, Dublin)
Ferdinand von Prondzynski	President, Dublin City University

Index